Bricks to Clicks

I0003429

"Scanlan's Bricks to Clicks is very readable and fu.
He has a wonderful way of making web fundamentals obvious and showing
how obvious facts are fundamental. He also graciously reminds us to use the
things we know and periodically forget."
    —   John Castle PhD, Lecturer in Entrepreneurship at Seattle University

"Bricks to Clicks is a timely read for anyone interested in navigating through
the maze of today's Internet opportunities. Scanlan delivers a stark and incisive
companion to the world of online business and entrepreneurship. It is
immediately accessible to both novice and geek through use of clear straight-
talking style and breadth of knowledge. This book will save time and money
and much angst for the website startup."
    —   Kieran O'Mahony PhD. Fellow of the Royal Geographic Society.
Owner, Educare Press (educarepress.com)

"Scanlan shows you how and why the real payoff from your website is not by
way of overnight success, but from long term devotion to content and customer
value, which reflects my own experience exactly ... right on target."
    —   Chris Folgmann - Owner, Light Matters (lmatters.com).

"... a highly practical and easy to understand roadmap for small and medium
size businesses as they contemplate a more effective Internet presence . ... a
strategic imperative for anyone at the beginning stages of using both the
Internet and Social Media for engaging prospects and customers."
    —   Jim Thornton, CEO Botanical Laboratories (botlab.com)

"Complexity is simplified and the web untangled in Scanlan's latest gem. Don't
buy this unless you have room for a successful website in your life. "
    - Christopher Sharpe , Accident and Injury Law (sharpelawfirm.org)

"A must-read for those who want to start a web presence or reinvigorate their
stagnant website."
    —   Henry J. McCabe – Owner, Golf Shot Fix (golfshotfix.com)

"Bricks to Clicks makes it so easy to understand how to generate leads on the
Web for a traditional bricks-and-mortar business."

    —   Julie Glassmoyer, Owner Sound Reflexology (soundreflexology.com)

"concise ... easy to follow ... gets right to the heart of the matter ... refreshingly
honest ... sound advice that works ... A must have book for anyone really
serious about creating a visible online presence."

    —   Lori Baratta, Owner, Lori Baratta Art Studios
(www.PartyFavorWebsite.com)

Bricks to Clicks

Bricks to Clicks

How to expand your small business profitably onto the Internet

Table of Contents

Bricks to Clicks

To every one of my clients, who walked with me every step on this journey of discovery

Bricks to Clicks

Introduction

I am in the business of getting my clients established profitably on the Internet and I start here with a confession:

Not all of my clients have succeeded on the web.

At least, in terms of their original expectations, they have not succeeded. A couple might even be a little angry with me. Throughout the process of delivering and executing each website project, my clients and I have learned a lot and, looking back on the last five years in particular, I see a pattern. The successful clients had something in common, and the *unsuccessful* clients also had something in common.

All of my clients are small-to-medium sized businesses, each working without a strong corporate brand to help them sell their product or service. In other words, they have to sell their product or service without the benefit of being instantly recognized in the marketplace, even if the products they sell have established brands.

What is the difference between the successful ones and the unsuccessful ones? The successful ones all focused their web presence efforts on *lead generation.* The unsuccessful ones focused their website presence efforts on *sales*.

The successful ones processed the leads generated by their website and, one-by-one, converted a percentage of them into sales. Over time, that grew into a loyal following and a valuable brand.

The unsuccessful ones – at least, until they changed their focus back to lead generation – paid little attention to generating leads on their website, but offered their products directly for sale, usually complete with shopping cart and credit card handling solutions like PayPal or Google Checkout. For the potential buyer arriving at the website, the physical act of making a purchase was pretty easy. The problem was, strangers visiting my client's website didn't want to buy online from them. At least, not without developing a relationship first.

The temptation is to believe that sales on eBay (or your physical store) will automatically translate into sales on your new website. After all, if you have the same company name and the same products, shouldn't a nicer experience on a dedicated website produce sales?

The problem is – in this second decade of the 21st century – people are reluctant to buy from an online company they do not recognize. They might find a bargain priced iPod on your acmeproducts4you.com website, but unless they recognize the seller – you – it is unlikely they will make a purchase. They will only buy from you after you establish a relationship with them. Your website might be a work of art; it might offer lots of valuable information, special offers and a community of like-minded shoppers, but if the buyer *does not recognize you*, it is unlikely you will make a sale. A six month-old website can't compete with a brand as strong as eBay's. eBay's brand strength, voluminous web traffic, and huge spread of available products together mean that it can charge significant fees for those wishing to avail of that power.

Looking at the website of any of my *successful* clients, I see a clear and welcoming way to get in contact with the business. That is what a website does when it is focused on generating leads. It is a combination of any of the following:

(a) a visual representation of the prospect being satisfied,

(b) an easy-to-find toll-free telephone number,

(c) possibly an offer of something for free,

(d) plenty of valuable and/or interesting information and

(e) an easy way to enter contact details.

Details on how to create an effective Target Landing Page can be found on page 36.

Increased competition

About ten or fifteen years ago, when the Internet was a lot younger, people were more willing to enter their credit card details into an unfamiliar website. Novelty and excitement drove them to it, unmitigated by fear of "identity theft" or bogus merchants or merchandise.

Not so today.

Today, people are far more cautious, and for good reason. They are willing to pay a higher price on a website like Amazon.com than for the same product on an unfamiliar website. It is because of the power of corporate brand, of course, and it brings us to the rule: *People are reluctant to make a purchase on a website with an unfamiliar corporate brand.*

People are reluctant to make a purchase on a website with an unfamiliar corporate brand

The problem is mitigated where the buyer has little alternative (e.g. you are selling overnights at a Bed & Breakfast in a sought-after location).

You might be selling highly recognized products – anything from *iPods* to *Tag Heuer* watches – but *it is the brand of the store owner* that counts with Web sales, and less the brand of the product. For example, you might be able to sell a Swiss Army knife on eBay for a reasonable sum, but not get any offers for it on your own website, even if you are able to attract significant visitor traffic to your website. The reason is, on eBay, each sale is implicitly *underwritten by eBay,* with all the support and purchase security that such a store implies.

What does all that mean to you, the small business owner who is expecting a return on the investment in your new website? It means you must, at the beginning, invest time in each new prospect relationship. You must use your website to *generate leads* – which may be as simple as inviting them to pick up a phone and call you – and develop a relationship with them. This is called the *Invitation to Engage,* which is covered on page 37. Over time, this relationship-building process builds your brand loyalty – either on a relationship-by-relationship basis or within your target market – to the point where sales will indeed occur on your website. In the early stages of developing your web presence, your website is focused on the *generation of leads*.

Bricks to Clicks

Building a brand on the Internet takes years, but generating leads on the Internet can begin almost immediately

It sounds like an arduous task, all this time and effort invested in "sucking up to strangers" as an old sales acquaintance of mine put it, but companies with real value are built that way in the early stages: one customer at a time, year after year.

We've all heard the overnight success stories of folks who set up on the Internet; people who published a simple website and made a fortune selling their wares. (I've never actually met one of these people in person, but I've heard a lot of stories). Those happy days of easy sales on the Internet are long gone, if indeed they ever existed. Today, it takes time – *years* – to build that "river of sales" as one of my clients put it.

To explain what is required to make sales on the web, I use the metaphor of a forest: you buy and plant saplings, followed by weeding and pruning. Beyond that, assuming your young forest gets enough sun and rain, the chief ingredient is *time*. No amount of money or resources will build a forest overnight, unless you want to buy and plant mature trees, of course, in which case the investment is prohibitively expensive. One difference between growing a forest and growing your business on the 'net is, in the case of your business, the 'planting' goes on indefinitely. In fact, on your new website, you must plant new material in it every day. More on that later.

The more things change ...

Of the billion or so websites on the Internet, the vast bulk of them have been lying dormant – unchanging, static – for years. They get few if any visitors and sit passively among a sea of stagnant websites. Even established businesses can have websites that sit there for years, never changing. And the irony is, the solution can be described simply. But it does take an uncommon discipline to actually do what is necessary: a*dd content to a website every day.*

> *For a website to grow in value, new content must be added every day*

In a traditional retail business – sometimes called a 'bricks-and-mortar' business – you can open a storefront, especially if it is in the right location, and customers show up almost immediately. If you have a popular brand (e.g. Starbucks), your new store (or café) might even open to full capacity on the very first day. You probably know by now that a website storefront doesn't work like that. Unless you inject a lot of money into advertising and other types of promotion, a new website takes time to draw in its first customers.

If you already have a profitable business – a bricks-and-mortar business, that is – you presumably know how to sell your product or service; you know how to talk about what you offer and – if you sell a variety of products – you know which are the most popular and which are the most profitable products. All that knowledge translates nicely into how you capture customers and/or prospects on your website. If you are already in business, it's going to be an easier, more predictable journey for you to reach profitability on the Internet.

On the other hand, if you have never sold what you are about to try and sell on the Internet, you have significant challenges ahead.

Still, it's not impossible – you can build a new business from scratch on the Internet – it is just harder if you don't already have a bricks-and-mortar business to base it on.

So, if you accept the assertion that making sales directly off your website – without developing a relationship/brand with a customer – is difficult, we arrive at the primary purpose of the website for almost every small business:

The primary purpose of a website for the vast majority of small businesses is to generate leads

For established brands (for example, British Airways, Walmart, Apple or Amazon.com), the primary purpose of a website is usually to *sell product*. These companies already have a well-known brand; but because your brand is unknown, your website's purpose will be less about selling product directly, and more about *gathering the contact details of prospective customers*, which is the process of lead generation.

The new way to generate leads

In the past half decade or so, the average business website has evolved from being a tactical, passive component of the business to being a strategic necessity. Today, prospective customers look at a business's website as a kind of "signature" of the company that owns it. A mediocre website implies a mediocre company. A professional website implies a professional organization.

Before a stranger becomes a customer, they must become a lead. Today, that is done through a website, so the need to have an effective website is imperative.

Most small business owners I know are aware that, sooner or later, they will have to pay serious attention to establishing their business on the web, if indeed they are not already on that journey. But where do they start? To make matters even more urgent, competition to appear early in search results has gotten decidedly tougher since the latest recession began in 2008.

With a strong emphasis on how to drive quality traffic to your website, the hard lessons of nearly two decades of delivering web solutions to small business are examined here. The clients I draw my experience from range from an established, one-person Reflexologist to a dozen-strong team of entrepreneurs wishing to take a bold new, high-tech product to market. Together, we built shopping basket solutions, image galleries, white papers, blogs, animations, questionnaires, social media integration and all manner of functionality using a variety of technologies inside web pages and on servers. Each client project focused on generating website traffic from search engines and gathering contact information from those visitors. A few of my clients focused their website on actual sales generation, essentially skipping the process of lead generation.

The easy part: understanding the technology

This book is written for the non-technical small business owner who wishes to establish a profitable web presence using their existing business – or business idea – as a foundation. I do use the occasional technical term, but I also explain everything in non-technical, business terms. For example, rather than asking *how does a Content Management System work*, I will talk about *how a Content Management System adds value to your business*.

One beautiful aspect of the Internet is that no one piece of it is difficult to understand. Yes, it is made up of many, many little pieces of technology, but no one element could be characterized as "rocket science". I say this to encourage you. Don't let the sound of any of it put you off. It's just not that complicated. In addition, there are many seasoned tools on the market that help you get active on the Internet quickly, including getting your first website published in a matter of hours or even minutes.

Some time around 2005, the breadth of technologies that made up the Internet seemed to settle. Although new "Social Media" choices, iPhone applications and all manner of search features come at us on a daily basis, the fundamentals have not changed much since Al Gore invented the Internet[1]. Even Social Media has not changed the underlying technology of what they call Internet Protocol (IP, is how stuff is sent back and forth across the

1   Likely for political purposes, Al Gore was misquoted in 2005 as having said he had "invented the Internet". I doubt that he ever said it, but it made for good political humor.

Internet, just like English is the language they use to communicate in air traffic control). If you managed a B on your math paper in high school, you'll understand everything you'll need to know – from a technical standpoint – about exploiting the Internet to expand your existing business.

The hard part: building a brand

At the risk of over-talking this point, success on the web requires that you establish a brand, and that takes both time and money. You will sell goods or services on your website to the degree you have established your brand. Newcomers to the web are shocked when eight months have gone by and they have not sold a darn thing on their new website, but the reason for zero sales is almost always the same: *they have not established a brand.*

Establishing a brand is ferociously expensive. It takes both time and money. Lots of it. If you have more time than money, you can do a lot of the leg-work yourself, nurturing each customer, one at a time, over a period of years, while you establish your brand.

Establishing a nationally recognized brand (or a global brand) is also a lot more expensive than establishing a local brand. "Local" in this context means "within driving distance". In other words, if your target market lives within ten miles or so, your market is "local". It is a lot cheaper to develop a brand in a local market because (1) you are targeting a much smaller number of people and (2) you have relatively limited competition.

Just how much more difficult is it to develop a national brand? Establishing a *national* brand can be several orders of magnitude more expensive than establishing a *local* brand. If you are selling, oh, let's say a product that stops leaves from clogging people's roof gutters, you will likely need to establish a national brand. It might cost millions of dollars to develop that national brand, because your market covers about a hundred million home owners, even if you limit your market to the United States. If you are trying to sell your tax preparation services to your local community, it might be mostly a question of time and work (and not so much money) to establish your brand. In the latter case, you can still expect it to take time before the first customers/clients pay you for your services. Establishing a brand in your local community will involve connecting with people through events and Social Media[2], and tying it all together through your website.

And so, the need to establish a brand before you can sell anything has not changed just because we are now selling on the Internet. Tempting as it is to believe a spanking new website will drive cash straight into your company's bank account, in truth, it will take time. Give it at least a year of adding content every day, and developing your brand in your market every day, before you judge your success, even if you experience some sales early in that effort.

Three stages, three skills

The life cycle of a sale on your website has three distinct stages. Two of the stages are done primarily by your

---

2   Social Media: Facebook, Twitter, others...

website and related web activities. The last one is often done person-to-person, at least at the beginning.

I break out these three stages because each requires a different skill:

1. Attract
2. Engage
3. Close

You must *Attract* visitors to your website, then *Engage* them when they get there so they give you their contact information and finally, *Close* business after you have developed a relationship with them. More on this topic on page 93.

It doesn't usually all happen in an afternoon of course. In fact, the whole process may take months and perhaps years to go through a complete cycle. Some sales may trickle in at the beginning – simply as a result of big numbers in your marketplace – but overnight success is rare.
Was it ever any other way!

> *What is Search Engine Optimization (SEO)?*
> *Search Engine Optimization is the actions you take*
> *to increase the chances your website will appear at*
> *the top of organic search results*

> *What does Organic mean?*
> *In the context of search results, organic means*
> *search results that are not advertisements*

SEO (Search Engine Optimization[3]) work is done mostly in the first – that is, the *Attract* – stage. Attraction drives visitors to your website. The more you get this part right, the more people will be looking at your website.

To *Engage* the visitors you have attracted means captivating them with something valuable enough (free, entertaining, educational, exciting news, or all of the above) so they volunteer their contact information. On an effective small company website, you will need a mechanism for gathering that contact information so it can be used later to stay in touch with those same visitors. Both the 'captivation' and the 'gathering' are central to the *Engage* stage, and require different skills to the *Attract* stage.

The *Attract* stage requires technical SEO skills. The *Engage* stage requires marketing skills, and the *Close* stage is a challenge in salesmanship. Thus, a successful web presence exploits the skills of an Engineer, a Marketer and a Salesperson.

---

3 Search Engine Optimization: the actions you take to make your website appear early in search results when people search for what you do.

A successful web presence exploits the skills of an Engineer, a Marketer and a Salesperson

It is common for a business to succeed in the first two stages and fail in the third; the *Close* stage. The Close stage requires the skill of *selling*. You have the prospect's attention, you control the conversation, and the time will come when you must *Ask for the Order*.

Fail early, fail often

My friend and professional salesperson Ross tells me that the reason eighty percent of all salespeople don't make it in sales is because they *can't ask for the order*. We've all been there. You've made your presentation, the prospect loves the story, the right people are in the room and … you shake hands and leave, promising to "get back to them later" about one open issue or another. So, instead of saying *"Can I go back to my office with a purchase order from you today, Ms. Henderson?"*, you postpone a potentially unpleasant answer and miss an opportunity to *Close the Deal* there and then. That is, to sell your valuable product to a person who actually wants it.

A real prospect *wants* to be sold to. They have remained engaged with you because they (probably) like you personally and they need your product.

A *pseudo*-prospect (sometimes called a "tire-kicker") will never buy from you, which is all the more reason you should *ask for the order today* and move on to something else the moment you discover they will not buy. Asking for the order now, when the time is right, is a great way of flushing out those time-wasting pseudo-prospects. "Fail early", as they say in sales circles, and spend the time instead with existing customers, real prospects, or going to a movie. At the very least, you'll save some of your precious time when you limit the time you waste with pseudo-prospects.

Timing is everything

There is an optimal time to ask for the order, of course, just like there is an optimal time to ask your steady girlfriend/boyfriend to marry you. Failure to get that timing right is to risk losing the opportunity to someone else. You might be the hottest date in town, but when it comes to marrying time, a woman (or a man) may opt for a solid proposal from Johnny Almost-as-Good than a *possible* proposal from Mister Hot-but-Hesitant. There are stacks of books on how to sell, so I'll leave it at this: Be bold; Ask for the Order.

It's the same on the Internet. At some point you have to *ask for the order*. The prospect found you, they like you, and are still subscribed to your monthly newsletter six months later, mostly as a result of their experience of what you have shared with them in six great issues of your newsletter. Now it is time to offer your product to them. It might be on the first page of the latest edition of your Newsletter, it might be a phone call or it might be a lone email offering them a great, special deal. I can't tell you when that right time is in your particular business case or what the offer should be, but timing deserves consideration.

Some businesses are cyclical – you might be selling yoga retreats in the Caribbean – in which case the timing of *asking for the order* will depend on the season of the year. Other sales opportunities are event-driven. If you are selling Team USA soccer gear, the week following the day the US qualifies for the World Cup might be the best time to *ask for the order*. In the former, because the business cycle is so rigidly tied to the seasons, your *Attract* and *Engage* stages need to respect the times of the year when folks search for such a retreat. It may be in the depths of winter – perhaps during a cold snap – that people dream of getting away from it all and they go searching for a yoga retreat in Jamaica.

A friend of mine owns a small Mediterranean restaurant in the Seattle area. When the day's forecast suggests a temperature above seventy degrees, he displays ads for Greek salads. When it is below seventy degrees, he displays an ad for baked fish.

A company that markets Caribbean yoga retreats might ask for the order in a given city when the temperature drops to freezing. Be aware of the cycles of your prospect base.

Bricks to Clicks

Chapter 1 - Creating a world class web presence

Guns don't kill people; bullets do

A website is only as good as its content, no matter how fancy it looks and no matter how much you've spent on its design. A website is about content, the way a gun is about bullets.

One of my clients goes everywhere armed with a loaded gun. He says he is – to use the popular American euphemism – "packing heat". His gun fits snugly into a holster strapped to his ankle and it is fully loaded with real bullets. He called me late one night giving me grief because his new website wasn't getting the traffic he had expected, let alone, sales from that traffic. He was ready, once again, to pull the plug on the project.

So I visited his office the next day and asked him to take his gun out of its holster, remove the ammunition, point the gun at me and to pull the trigger. Even though the gun was not loaded at this point, my customer did not pull the trigger. (I was quite thankful for that, actually. I don't know enough about guns to know whether an unloaded one is still dangerous or not. Perhaps a single bullet was sitting in the chamber or something. Anyway, he didn't pull the trigger, and I was grateful).

He got the point. A gun is useless when it has no bullets in it. He needed to add content to his new website.

A website only comes alive when it has content. Just as a gun is useless without bullets, a website is a useless container without content.

A website is useless without content

Time and time again, I see daily new content – meaning, at least one new page added to the same website every day – produce significantly higher positions in search results for a website.

Daily new content produces a significantly higher position in search results

Back in 2006, a friend of mine asked me, *hey Liam, how do I get traffic to my blog*? to which I answered, *write a new blog posting to it every day, and stick to your subject. About a year later, you'll see some traffic*, I told him. That was quite a few years ago – before I took up SEO as an exclusive specialization – but the rules have not changed much since then. At that time, I was speaking from a gut feeling and some strong anecdotal evidence; today, I am saying it because I have seen it happen on dozens of my clients' websites.

Of itself, having the content on the website is not enough. It has to include new material – that is, brand new published pages – every day[4]. You may have hundreds or even thousands of pages on your website, but if new pages are

---

4   If not every day, then almost every day. For the purposes of simplicity, I recommend to my clients that they publish new content to their website every day.

not published every day, your website will slip from the top of search results.

Just two days ago, I was looking at the Google Analytics reports relating to website traffic of one of my clients. Over the past eighteen months or so, my client has been gradually adding to their website the thousand or so products they have been selling for years in their bricks-and-mortar store. In that time, there were two periods of about two or three months when they did not add anything at all – in other words, no new content got published on their website during each brief period of no new content – and sure enough, you could see the traffic chart drop about a month after content addition paused, and then pick up again once they continued their product upload process. The small screen shot of the report can be seen in Illustration 1 on page 30.

It makes sense, doesn't it, that search engines would favor websites with a demonstrated history of adding fresh content. Such a website suggests an active organization, and fresh content implies novelty, a characteristic of valuable information on the Web.

It is said that the *value of information lies in its unusualness*. If that's true, it makes complete sense that search engines would favor websites with daily fresh content.

Still, no matter how often I draw attention to the need for new content, people appear not to believe me. Perhaps it comes across as a "take two aspirin and call me later" suggestion, where the website owner feels I am simply trying to get them to stop bothering me. Or maybe it is because adding new content every day takes extraordinary discipline.

An acquaintance of mine was annoyed with his company's website's performance. *How come the company they hired to build their website didn't drive the kind of sales their competitor in town got from their website?* he asked me.

A quick examination determined the answer. His own website had a few products for sale, and his competitor had

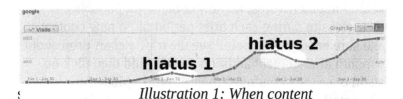

Illustration 1: When content addition pauses, web traffic soon drops off

Perhaps more importantly, the competitor was diligent at adding new products every day. Between the vast number of pages and the daily addition of new content, the competitor was way ahead of the game, at least in the eyes of search engines. It would be a long time before my acquaintance's employer's website would catch up.

But, adding content is expensive! my acquaintance exclaimed. He said it would be too expensive for him to add so much content.

Here's another thing about content. It is the gift that keeps on giving. In the case of the competitor's website above, new products were being added daily, and when a given piece was sold, it was simply marked as "sold", but left on the website, where it could attract for all eternity visitors searching for similar products. Again, you have to think in the longest terms possible. Forget about getting rich quickly on the Web. The Web rewards only those with a long term strategy.

You reap what you sow. And sowing in your website means adding content to it regularly. If you don't sow anything, you won't be reaping anything. I will cover this in more detail in the chapter on ROI (Return on Investment) on page 134.

Increasing the value of a website

Don't worry about getting every last typo out of each blog posting you are adding to your website. As I covered earlier, the trick to blog postings is to get them up and published every day. The more time you spend on perfecting each posting, the more likely you are to drop the activity altogether. Later, if certain blog postings are generating a lot of traffic or interest, you can go back and edit the grammar and spelling, or expand the blog posting if you wish.

> *Don't spend more than about ten minutes on a blog posting before publishing it*

If your Content Management System offers the feature to auto-publish a page at a specified time and date in the future, consider doing a year's worth of blog postings within a short period of time. Schedule each posting to be published at the same time of each day, publishing only one posting on each day.

I find this method effective because you can focus on blog postings all at one time – even though it might take a couple of weeks to do a whole year's worth – rather than having to come back to it once a day, re-focusing your mind back to blogging every time.

> *Consider doing a year's worth of blogging in a single sitting. That way, it is more likely to get done*

When you have all 365 blog postings lined up on auto-publish for the next twelve months, you will have satisfied one of the core requirements for high positioning in search results. That requirement is *regular new content*. Even if you don't do anything else to your website, that new content every day will work for you every day. Also, a year's worth of new content will give you some good website traffic to analyze for search words being used.

Let's recap what this chapter is all about.

Developing a web presence is a long term project. Think in terms of years, not months. It takes time and attention to get that new website established to the point where it is "taking care of itself". In the meantime, adding daily, relevant, quality content is the central most important factor in ensuring your long term success.

What is a blog?

The word "blog" is short for "web log" or weblog. The concept of a blog was born, sometime in the early 1990s, when people began writing their thoughts or journals on their own websites. Some grew into fully-fledged news services and centers for the dissemination of information to interested people. Others became a lucrative point for displaying online advertising. Blogs have become a strategic element of many organizations' web presence.

A blog can be an excellent way of driving search traffic to you, particularly if it (1) sticks to the subject, (2) new postings are added daily and (3) it contains information a lot of people are actually interested in.

More and more, a company's blog is an integral part of its website. In other words, both the website and the blog use the same domain name. A domain name is the part of the web address that an organization owns. Microsoft.com, ibm.com, bbc.co.uk, uspto.gov, are all examples of domain names. In my own company, my website lives at www.siteleads.net and my blog lives at www.siteleads.net/bm/blog. Having both together helps increase search traffic to my website because it concentrates the content value of both into a single website, making it more effective than the sum of both when each is taken separately.

Another way to concentrate the value of a website and a blog is to place the blog in a subdomain of the website. An example of a subdomain is blog.siteleads.net. Very loosely speaking – and I can feel my engineer friends cringing when I say this – if a domain were a city, then a subdomain would be a suburb within that city. Wikipedia describes a subdomain as *a domain that is part of a larger domain*. In other words, blog.siteleads.net is a domain that is part of the larger siteleads.net domain.

It is critically important, by the way, to own the primary domain name upon which you build your website and invest in content generally. I go into this critical topic in detail in the chapter on Intellectual Property on page 167.

> *It is critically important that you own the domain name your website is built upon*

Effective blog postings

Many years ago, I met a film director on a plane and he told me that a good film doesn't have anything in it that doesn't feed the point of the movie. He said, *if there's a boy crossing the street in the background of a scene, it must be part of the story*, however remote the connection might be. It might be that the movie is set in the 1970s, so the boy has a "John Travolta haircut" to support the period the movie was set in, or that the director is trying to portray the setting as a safe neighborhood by showing a young boy walking through it, and so on. He said, *every leaf on every tree supports the movie. If it's not relevant, remove it. The more you can do that, the better the movie will be.* Unless it is an enormously high-budget movie, you can't remove everything irrelevant from the set of course, especially if it is being shot in a public place, but you get the point. The more relevant the content of the blog posting to what you are promoting on your website, the more effective it will be.

In most cases, a daily blog posting to your website is one of the most effective and long-lasting ways of driving targeted traffic to your website. When it is done right, of course.

Bricks to Clicks

Whether you are talking about directing a movie, writing poetry, pastel portraiture or writing a love song, *the art of it is in the elimination of all things irrelevant.*

> *The art of writing a blog entry is in the elimination of all things irrelevant*

So what does that mean with respect to blog postings? It means, an effective blog posting is 1. a few sentences long (because it only takes a paragraph to make a point) and 2. everything in it is 100% relevant to the point you are trying to make.

This is good news, because if you are going to write a blog posting for every day of the year, knowing that it needs to be short comes as a bit of a relief.

People often worry about having perfect spelling and punctuation in their blog posting. There is no harm done when all your "i's are dotted and your t's are crossed", but the essence of the blog posting is that it is done quickly. It is a sketch, a quick idea, a brief opinion. You can always come back later and clean up the text in any blog posting that attracts web traffic. And that brings us to the whole point of having lots of small blog entries. Each one is like its own lottery ticket. The more you have, the more chances you have of winning something. What is the prize? Web traffic.

Other pages on your website may take a lot more care and attention to produce. Yesterday, I spent about five hours writing a page on my website that spoke about the service my company offered. That page was more like a "White Paper", detailing an aspect of my business that must be described thoroughly and unambiguously. But a blog posting can be short.

Effective Target Landing Pages

You never get a second chance to make a first impression

A Target Landing Page[5] (TLP) is the page a visitor will see on your website when they arrive on that website for the first time. The visit may be a consequence of a blog posting they read, an advertisement you placed on the Internet, a matching set of search words to keywords, a link from another website, a radio ad, a link provided by a friend, a suggestion in Facebook, or other source. The objective of a TLP is to convert a visitor into a lead.

> *The purpose of a Target Landing Page is to convert a visitor into a lead*

To convert a visitor into a lead requires that the TLP capture the imagination of the visitor, usually in a matter of seconds, and convince them the website has something they want or need. The TLP has succeeded when the visitor has given you their contact information. In other words, when the visitor becomes a lead.

---

5   There is also a type of TLP known as the *Secondary* Target Landing Page, which I go into on page 45

Bricks to Clicks

Your Target Landing Page has succeeded when the visitor has given you their contact information

How do you capture the visitor's imagination and convince them they are in the right place? A very common method of doing both is to present a free and attractive offer of something on the TLP. For example, on Netflix's TLP (their Home Page), they offer a full month of free movie rentals to anyone who signs up on the spot. On a nursing training course website, I saw an offer for "one free course" (valued at $49) to the visitor, when they sign up for free on the spot.

An Invitation to Engage

Giving something of value away for free is often very much worth it. A month of free movie rentals doesn't cost Netflix so much – perhaps a few dollars – and is without a doubt a very cost effective way of capturing leads. I can only believe, a majority of leads captured by Netflix this way ultimately turn into paying customers.

Offering something of value to a visitor in exchange for their contact information is an *Invitation to Engage*.

Considering the core purpose of a website in a small company is to *generate leads*, the effectiveness of the TLP is clearly critical. When a visitor lands on one of your TLPs, you have, quite literally, *a few seconds* to capture their attention with your message, or they will be gone.

Most visitors to most TLPs I have seen (when I examine the Google Analytics reports behind them) leave within a few seconds. That is because it is difficult to capture visitors' attention and most people struggle to succeed with it.

Common design mistakes on a TLP

1. There is no clear *Invitation to Engage*.

2. There are too many irrelevant or distracting elements.

3. It is not clear what product or service is on offer.

4. A visitor cannot "see themselves satisfied" on the TLP.

Considering your current Target Landing Page, can you answer Yes to the following questions:

1. Is the visitor presented with an obvious and easy *Invitation to Engage*?

2. Does everything on the page relate to the visitor or the *Invitation to Engage*?

3. Is it clear what your product or service is?

4. Does it contain a visual representing your target customer?

Show me Me

It is hard to believe, but many companies spend vast sums of money on online advertising only to confuse the new visitor with a unclear or missing message on the Target Landing Page. Often, the first thing you read on a TLP is about the company itself. For example: *Acme Siding Products of Wisconsin has been in business since 1972*. When a new visitor arrives on your TLP, the first thing they want to see is *themselves*, not you. This is the *Show me Me* principle. Netflix's TLP shows a picture of a family gathered around their home TV. That family is Netflix's target market, so when such a visitor arrives there, *they see themselves being satisfied*, not Netflix. Imagine if they landed on the Netflix TLP and they saw a picture of a Netflix's sorting facility with the caption *We are the biggest DVD rental company in the world*. Impressive as all that looks and sounds, it is misplaced when it is on the TLP. Visitors care little about you and your company – at least, not until you have developed a relationship with them – but they sure are interested in themselves.

One of the first things I look for on the TLP is *people*. Is there an image of a person or people on your TLP? Often, the page has a picture of the corporation's headquarters – a large, impressive building perhaps – with not a single human being in sight. Only this morning, I looked up the website of a pharmaceuticals business on the east coast of the US. Sure enough, it showed a picture of their main office. I also looked up a hotel website developed by a highly qualified software engineer. The (supposed) Target Landing Page had a set of revolving photographs of inside and outside the hotel. They must have gone to great lengths to avoid showing people in the photographs because, sure enough, the hotel appeared deserted. There was an empty hotel lobby, an empty restaurant, rooms, corridors, grounds and reception. If it were stills from a movie, that movie would be titled *When the Humans Disappeared*.

Empty places are rarely welcoming, unless you are selling a solitary, desert island experience.

Always show an image of a person or people in your TLP

Very roughly speaking, about one-third of the space used on a Target Landing Page is taken up with an image of the *Show Me Me* variety and two-thirds of the space is taken up with the *Invitation to Engage*.

The Relationship

Anyone with a natural gift for developing relationships has a distinct advantage in this new Social Media driven business on the Web. The final step in the cycle of generating business is still to *generate revenue*, but relationship development has never been as important to business as it is today.

To summarize, an effective Target Landing Page invites the visitor to *begin a relationship* with your organization. It provides the means to do that by offering, for example, *free movie rentals* in exchange for the visitor's credit card and contact details, or *access to the forum's expert service*, or *the first week of home delivery meals for free with a monthly sign-up*. Whatever the particulars of your product or service, something of value is offered in exchange for the visitor's contact information. Providing that information to you *turns the visitor into a lead*.

Offering something of value to become a customer (like offering a ten percent discount or a free box of chocolates with every purchase) is different from *offering something to become a lead*. When you do not have a strong store brand, you need to develop a relationship – that is, convert the visitor into a lead – before you try to sell them anything.

An effective Target Landing Page invites the visitor to begin a relationship with your organization

What is Bounce Rate?

The percentage of visitors that arrive on a Target Landing Page and go away without visiting any other page on the website is called the Bounce Rate. As an initial objective with my own clients' websites, I aim to *simply reduce the Bounce Rate as much as possible*. A Bounce Rate of 75% on one type of website might be acceptable, while a 40% Bounce Rate on another might be a poor result. As we progress through the project of developing my client's web presence, we will adjust our target bounce rate and watch how it changes as we change the contents of the Target Landing Page.

The more effective your Target Landing Page is at capturing the attention of that first-time visitor, the lower your Bounce Rate, and the higher the chance a given visitor will convert into a lead.

When is a high Bounce Rate OK?

The nature of the product or service being offered on a Target Landing Page, as well as countless market conditions, will determine what a "good" or "bad" Bounce Rate will be. Netflix, with their "cheap and simple" offering may regard a 50% Bounce Rate as too high. On the other hand, Airbus Industries may consider a 95% Bounce Rate as excellent, when they consider the millions of airplane nuts (me among them) that will click any link that contains a reference to airplanes in it.

> *When it reflects the filtering out of tire-kickers, a*
> *higher Bounce Rate is sometimes a good thing*

If your TLP is ineffective at generating leads but good at keeping visitors' attention, you may get a low Bounce Rate (good) but also a low visitor-to-lead conversion ratio (bad). If the only thing a new visitor can do on a TLP (Target Landing Page) is accept the special offer and input their contact details, the page could have a high Bounce Rate, but can be *excellent* at generating quality leads. This is a subtlety that also applies to sales. As I mention elsewhere in this book (page 24) with respect to shepherding a prospect through the sales pipeline, it is also good to "fail early" at the lead generation stage. In the context of visitors to the Target Landing Page, "failing early" means weeding out visitors we determine will never become customers. That principle works just as well with visitors to your website. There are ways to determine quickly if a visitor is ever going to become a customer. Offering them a "sign up or go away" choice on the Target Landing Page is often enough to do just that. These pseudo-prospects (or tire-kickers) waste your time. The sooner they go away, the better.
I talk a little more on the topic of "fail early" with respect to sales on page 24.

How do you measure your Bounce Rate?

Many websites today have included inside their website a product called Google Analytics. It is a free – and truly excellent – piece of software provided by Google that allows you to track visitor behavior on your website, including Bounce Rate. With Google Analytics (GA), you can see the Bounce Rate for your website as a whole, for an individual page, or for any number of other selected sections of your website. I won't go into all the possibilities of GA here, because to do so would require another thousand pages. Suffice it to say, Google Analytics should be installed in any website that is contributing to your business. Using GA to monitor specific Target Landing Pages' Bounce Rates allows you to continuously fine-tune your message on those pages.

Netflix: An example of an effective Target Landing Page

It is likely you have heard of Netflix. Netflix is a true marvel of the Internet, and it is no surprise then that they have done what appears to be an excellent job of their Primary Target Landing Page: their Home Page.

If you are a customer of Netflix, and you have already signed into their website at least once, you may not be able to see their Primary Target Landing Page easily, because browsing to their Home Page (www.netflix.com) will redirect you to a page for existing customers. If you are a customer, there is no need for them to try to "capture you as a lead", so you will be steered away from their Target Landing Page. It might even log you in automatically if you have saved your login id and password. How do they know you are a customer? The last time you logged into the Netflix website, your browser stored visitor information on your PC, so it would know you are a returning customer.

Netflix dedicates their Home Page to be their Primary Target Landing Page for potential new customers. Everything on that one page focuses on the single purpose of harvesting visitors into leads, by offering them an attractive, limited-time free offer. No money changes hands when the visitor signs up for the free offer, but the process develops the visitor into such a strong lead, they automatically become a paying customer when the "free period" expires a month later.

To be fair to all of us with our lesser-known brands, Netflix has such a strong brand, it is easier for them to ask visitors for their credit card information than it would be for you and me on our lesser known websites. In other words, the stronger the corporate brand, the more pushy the TLP can be in steering the visitor towards becoming a lead.

A known corporate brand allows a TLP to be more aggressive in converting a visitor into a lead

You and I don't have the brand leverage of Netflix, and because we don't, we must nurture each prospect relationship, and continue to do that until we have a strong enough brand for first-timers to our website to enter their credit card information. People trust companies like Amazon.com, Netflix and Google enough to give them their credit card details. That is the power of brand.

In terms of whom they need to trust, when people make a purchase on the web, they are buying from whatever the overarching organization is, not the brand of the product. For example, when someone buys something from your store on eBay, they are really buying from eBay, not from you. That is why new sellers on eBay can be up and selling product in no time. Creating your own corporate brand from scratch on the web is a huge challenge.

The connection between a blog and a Target Landing Page

Each blog posting on your website is a potential *Secondary Target Landing Page*, and as such, it has to do a little more work than just offer up a snippet of wisdom to your visitors. Typically, there is an *Invitation to Engage* displayed prominently at the top of this page. Thus, when a visitor arrives here for the first time, they are presented with the opportunity to become a lead.

A Secondary Target Landing Page (STLP) is not dedicated exclusively to the purpose of generating leads, because it must provide the information that the visitor was searching for to begin with, otherwise it would not have attracted the visitor in the first place.

We have all seen examples of Secondary Target Landing Pages (STLPs). Some are subtle, some are in-your-face, and it is often hard to find the actual piece of text you were seeking in the noise of self-serving ads and promotions crowding out the web page you have landed on.

Many websites don't actually offer any product or service of their own. Instead, they collect commissions on traffic they send to paying advertisers whose ads they display. This is called *Affiliate Marketing*. You've probably seen those types of websites. You search for something, click the first item in the list of search results, and you are brought to a website loaded down with ads.

Just how subtle you want your *Invitation to Engage* to be will depend on many factors, including your target market, product or service, competition, pricing and other factors. How that invitation should look is the subject of many, many other marketing books, and a much bigger subject than I could cover here. What I tell you is what I have learned are the common characteristics of successful Target Landing Pages – and also, common mistakes – on page 38.

In terms of how your own TLP might appear, I tend to look first at what the *successful players in the same market* are doing. Look at your competitors' websites. What kind of offers are they making? How do they describe their product or service value? How do they capture visitor contact information in their website?

The role of brand in Internet sales

People buy *brands*, not *products*, and brands only live in the minds of buyers. Even when there is a product with the same power of an iPod in the marketplace for a much lower price, the iPod's *brand* makes it a more valuable product. That is because they are buying the brand, not the product. Such is the power of brand!

In the physical world – that is, in a store on Main Street – a buyer is more willing to purchase a product when they see the physical store as underwriting the purchase. As the owner of a physical store on Main Street, you may not have the brand power of Bloomingdales, but your customer knows he or she can return to your store if there is an issue with their purchase. Your physical store implies a host of ways a customer can hunt you down when there is a problem. Your physical store gives you some brand value, even if it is not Bloomingdales. This is not the case when they make a purchase on the Web, where there is no such brand value.

When you make a purchase on the Web, there is no physical store to return to. You can buy a product online in a store that, a week later, has evaporated. And so, the would-be buyer pays more attention to the *store brand* on the Internet than they do in the physical world. If the would-be buyer does not recognize your store brand (For example, "Acme Plastic Products Inc.") you are less likely to make the sale. It's not impossible for you to make a sale, but – all else being equal – the weaker the brand of the online store, the *less likely* a visitor will make a purchase. Obvious as that may sound, most website owners proceed as if it were not true.

Illustration 2 on page 48 indicates the relative order of brand importance with respect to sales on the Internet.

The weaker the brand of the online store, the less likely a visitor will make a purchase

Illustration 2: Store brand trumps Seller brand

If you are selling products on eBay, it is the power of the eBay brand (the Store brand) that implicitly underwrites each sale you make, not the power of the your brand (whatever you call your store) which is a *Seller* brand within the greater eBay *Store*. In time, the strength of your (the seller's) brand within eBay will emerge, but at the beginning, sales will rely heavily on eBay's brand strength, not yours. This means that you can set up a store on eBay –

assuming your product is something people want – and start selling from the first day of business. On your new website, however, your store has no brand recognition yet, so it is likely going to be a while before a stranger makes a purchase without getting to know you first. Just how long will you have to wait before that first sale on your website? It depends. Some of my clients see their first such sale within weeks of publishing products on their new website; with others, it has taken many months. However long it takes, remember that the *brand strength of the store* is a critical factor of sales on the Web. Always remember the primary objective of the website of most small companies: *it is to generate leads,* not to generate sales directly.

It is so easy to underestimate the power of the store brand and to think that it is the seller and/or the product brands that are the driving force behind the sale. I see many a business owner conclude that their own seller brand is what powers their sales on eBay, only to discover later that it was the eBay brand that drove sales from the beginning.

Does a market exist for your product?

Selling the product vs. selling the requirement

Because everyone always answers that question with a resounding Yes, I like to ask the question a different way: *Are people <u>spending money today</u> solving the problem you solve*? If the answer is Yes, by definition there is a market for what you offer.

Whether you sell jewelry, offer a massage service, sell golf equipment or prepare tax returns, the question you must answer is, *are people <u>spending money today</u> solving the*

problem you solve? For each of the four offerings (jewelry, massage, golf and tax) the answer is Yes, at least in general terms. Put the traditional way, there is an *established market* for each of the four offerings. The challenge such a business faces then is to compete with other companies for customers who know what they want and have money to spend on it. Prospective customers in an existing market know what to expect, want what you've got and have already decided they will buy from one of the companies supplying to that market. This is called *Selling the Product* (versus *Selling the Requirement,* which I will go into, below). Knowing whether you are *selling the product* or *selling the requirement* will tell you how difficult the Close stage will be for you.
Here's why:

Selling the Product is the act of convincing the prospect that your offering is of greater value to your competitors' offerings. If you succeed in doing this (convincing the prospect your offering is the best available), you make the sale.

Selling the Requirement, on the other hand, is when you have a solution to a problem that no one knows they have. *Selling the Requirement* is a lot harder than *Selling the Product* for a number of reasons. First, you have to convince someone that they have a problem, after which they may or may not become a prospect (even if you convince them they have a problem, they might have no interest in paying money to solve it, or may go searching for an alternative to your solution). Then, even if they become a prospect (they are considering buying your offering), you still have to sell them your product. You can see, there is a far greater cost associated with convincing people they have a problem, than simply selling them a solution to a problem they already know they have. This is the painful and costly process of creating a market. You might work on a hundred people who have the problem you solve, converting a mere five of them to believers, but those five still have not become leads. So, you can see how the math of the *Selling the Requirement* challenge is working against you.

On the other hand, when there is a market for what you offer (that is, you are *selling the product* not the requirement), by the time a prospect finds you, they may be close to becoming a customer.

I don't want to minimize the challenge of selling a product, but I know from personal experience, I never again want to sell a requirement for a living. Been there, done that, and I have scars to prove it.

An old friend of mine who has for decades made a good living in sales, said "the hardest thing to do in the world is change someone's mind". He was talking about *selling the requirement.*

I've had a number of prospective clients come to me with a product that was perhaps revolutionary – and impressive for many reasons – but there was no one out there who knew they had the problem it solved. So I knew I couldn't help them.

Even when people know they have a problem, they may not know there is a solution available. So they don't go looking for it. In addition – as many marketing professionals understand – people are more likely to make a purchase if there are alternatives. Seeing alternatives endorses the product category in the eyes of the purchaser, which increases the likelihood that they will make a purchase. This has got to do with the concept of *product category*, which I describe on page 53.

Some fifteen years ago, I read an article in the *Wall Street Journal* titled something like *What makes a CEO[6] successful?* At the top of the list was *"A market exists for what the company offers"*. It struck me how obvious the claim was and yet, how so many people in business ignore it. Certainly, the Wall Street Journal thought it necessary to point it out, and it was listed as the Number One contributing factor in a CEO's success. Just as the rooster believes his crowing causes the sun to rise at dawn, we humans often believe we have more of a hand in results than we actually do. When a market already exists for what we sell, we know – as roosters – the sun will at least rise. But I digress...

The "Market" vs. the "Marketplace"

Today, that same factor – *whether a market exists for what you offer* – is the biggest governor of how successful you will be on the web – or indeed in any business – so it is important to understand exactly what "a market exists" means in terms of the Internet. And so, you have the same question you need to answer, but with a twist: *Are people spending money <u>on the Internet</u> today solving the problem your company solves*?

---

6   CEO: Chief Executive Officer of a corporation

For you to succeed, people must already be spending money today <u>on the Internet</u> for a solution like yours

People are happy buying new socks from a department store, but will they buy socks online? I know I would not. For me, buying socks is a personal, touchy-feely thing. I need to pick them up, get a sense of how heavy they are, how soft the cotton is, and so on. I might even caress my cheeks with the socks before I make my purchase decision.

And so, we come to the difference between a *Market* and a *Marketplace*. There is clearly a huge *market* for socks. But their age-old *marketplace* – Department Stores – is different from the *marketplace* of the Internet, or the marketplace of eBay or Amazon.com. Obvious as it may sound, you need to be aware that some products do not translate well to the Internet. You must ask yourself the question again: *Are people spending money <u>on the Internet</u> today solving the problem you solve?*

The Product Category

I am a devoted student of the seasoned marketing professionals Al Ries and Jack Trout, whose publication *22 Immutable Laws of Marketing* I regard as my Ten Commandments when it comes to the subject of marketing. They talk in depth about something called the *Product Category*, but they don't really define what it is. Considering the critical role it plays in marketing on the web, I feel it needs a clear and unambiguous definition.

> *A product category is a commonly accepted list of
> similar potential solutions to a given problem*

By "similar" I mean the solutions on the list have a similar
price, solution and quality.

A buyer walks out his front door with a product category
written on a piece of paper. For example: If I want to buy a
reliable, modestly-priced SUV[7] with car-like fuel economy,
I may walk out the door with a list that contains the
following five cars:

(1) Honda CRV

(2) Toyota RAV4

(3) Ford Escape

(4) Subaru Forrester and

(5) Jeep Patriot

Can you easily identify the list of solutions in the product
category to which your product or service belongs? A lack
of real competition, while it smells like a huge opportunity,
suggests that no one will be looking for a solution like
yours, that there is no substantial market for what you have,
and that you might end up *selling the requirement* instead
of *selling the product.*

A key commonality among members of a Product Category
is price. It is rare that someone leaves the house with a
written list of potential products where one solution on the
list is twice the price of another on the list. Identifying the

---

7   Sport Utility Vehicle

price range of your solution's Product Category is therefore important to knowing if a market exists for what you sell.

Imagine a man leaving his family home to go shopping for that SUV. As he walks out the door, he says to his wife, "Honey, I may spend between $20,000 and $40,000 on the new SUV". You can see how such a comment might alarm his wife standing in the doorway. More likely, the man would have a list of alternatives, all of which were within about ten percentage points in price of one another. If fact, it is more likely that an originally more expensive, but *used* car now of a similar price will be on that shopping list. When two seemingly similar products have significantly different prices, it is more likely they do not belong to the same product category.

If you believe strongly that your product is similar to another product with a much different price, but you are still convinced you and they are true competitors, it is likely that your product category does not yet exist and that your market is not yet mature. Product Categories exist only in a mature market. In an *immature* market, prices tend to fluctuate a lot and vary considerably between competitors. In a mature market, potential buys know what to expect to pay for your product before you ever hear from them.

You need to know:

1. Whether you are *selling a requirement* or *selling a product*,

2. What Product Category your product or service belongs to and

3. What the price range is for members of your
    Product Category.

Building a brand from scratch on the Internet is not for the
faint-hearted, but convincing people on the web they have a
problem they don't yet understand (selling the requirement)
is for those who really enjoy pain.

The Gold Rush

Between 1848 and 1849, the population of San Francisco
grew from approximately one thousand to 25,000 full-time
residents. The reason for the increase was the California
Gold Rush, which began in 1848 and lasted about seven
years. A lucky few made a fortune in the Gold Rush, but
most returned home with "little more than they started
with[8]". People came from all over the world – as well as
from North America – to seek their fortune in the hills and
rivers of California and elsewhere. Some came over land,
others by sea; many risked life and limb to make the
journey.

The Internet Age of today is a bit like the Gold Rush of the
mid-nineteenth century.

We've all heard stories of people making a fortune on the
Internet. We are dazzled by tales of individuals "publishing
online stores and customers rushing in with their cash" or
start-up entrepreneurs getting "ten million dollars of
funding based on a five-slide PowerPoint presentation". We
stopped thinking straight, replacing sound business
reasoning with lofty dreams of instant fame and fortune

---

8   According to Wikipedia

delivered to our door by our dreamy startup. Just like in the Gold Rush of the nineteenth century, few experienced overnight success, but for the patient and disciplined – today just as much as over a century ago – there was a good living to be made. And for a small handful, a fortune.

Stories of success have drawn millions of bricks-and-mortar business owners – or would-be business owners – to the Internet, just as California drew hundreds of thousands in search of gold.

Imagine what it must have been like if you were one of the original prospectors – or one of the locals – when your town was overrun by so many newcomers, all hypnotized by Gold Fever! It's a bit like that on the Internet today. Every day or so, I get a phone call from a business owner looking for help, telling me that they used to appear at the top of search results but don't anymore. How did that happen, they ask me? It happened because a newcomer further up the river – if I may stretch the metaphor – is now sifting out the gold before it reaches the established website further down the river. Just like in the Gold Rush, where it took a few years for gold panning techniques to get sophisticated enough to push the incumbents aside, techniques for appearing on Page One of search results today have gotten more sophisticated and more competitive. In addition, the Great Recession that began in late 2008 added more urgency to the need for success on the Internet, because companies were losing revenue from their traditional channels. And so, the rush to the Internet became ever more urgent as revenue dried up back at the bricks-and-mortar store.

It is not the answer that enlightens, but the question.
- Eugene Ionesco

And so, droves of prospectors arrive on the Internet daily. Some arrive with few resources, while others are armed with the best shovels, pans and spades money can buy. Some companies spend fifty dollars on a website and expect it to support their ambitions of lead generation and business growth. Others throw millions of dollars into website development, online advertising, Social Media development and everything else, in a frantic effort to seize as much of the market as they can before someone else does. What is the right approach? It all depends on what you need to achieve. The answers are easy … if you ask the right questions.

Questions I wish I'd asked

A few years into my latest startup, Siteleads.net, I went back to my first dozen clients and asked them to tell me *what questions do they wish they had asked before the project started*. Understandably, I was a little uncomfortable approaching them with the request, but I was glad I did. How they replied was an education for me.

There was a commonality among each set of questions they gave me. Among each list of five questions, the same two questions kept appearing. Paraphrased, they were:

1. *how long will it take before I make money on the Internet*, and

2. *how much work do I have to do*?

I'll return to those questions a bit later. But first, I want to talk about how important it is for your company to appear at the top of search results.

In the year 1995, Microsoft and Netscape were engaged in a browser war (Internet Explorer vs. Netscape Navigator), and since then, there have been many such wars, won and lost, by new companies and old. Microsoft is still around of course, but there is no denying that Google holds the crown for control of a lot of what matters on the World Wide Web today, at least, as of typing this paragraph in 2011. So, when I talk about search engines, I use Google as a proxy for all search engines, because most other search engines emulate Google, and a lot of business on the Internet begins with a Google search. In fact, some eighty-five percent of business-to-business transactions begin today with a search[9].

The majority of all searches on the Internet are done in Google and a whopping seventy-five percent of Internet sales from searches begin their journey at one of the *first three organic[10] entries* on the *first page* of search results[11]. Of course, not all such sales happen immediately – few do, in fact – but the vast majority of ultimate sales on the web begin with a vendor's website appearing at the top of Page One of search results.

What does that mean to you, the business owner? It means, if your small business – or another entity selling your

---

9   According to MarketingSherpa

10 Organic: a search result that is displayed not as a result of advertising but because of content relevancy and related factors.

11 The unshaded area – sometimes called Organic Search Results - right below the ads that often appear at the top of search results.

product or service – never appears at the top of search results, you're missing a lot, and it may put you out of business. Sure, some businesses thrive on word-of-mouth (Tupperware) or pure brand strength (Coca-Cola), and there will always be such businesses around. But as the Internet reaches deeper and deeper into our lives – both business and personal – it is having an increasing influence on all elements of how we conduct business, and not just how we find products.

All is not lost. Your own website may not appear at the top of search results, but a company selling your product or service may. For example, if you sell secondhand sports memorabilia on your website, people searching for what you have, may see your eBay store selling it. You could call your presence on eBay "your store" but really, what is important is that eBay is so big, it is its own *marketplace* and it is *their* store we are talking about. This is an important distinction: the difference between *market* and *marketplace*. Whoever owns the domain name owns the intellectual property it contains, including its brand power. In terms of brand power, as we discussed earlier, eBay very definitely owns all the stores within their eBay domain (eBay.com), which is why they can charge a handsome amount for selling your product for you.

There are countless other examples of how the marketplace of the Internet behaves like a physical marketplace. You are reading a book you likely purchased in the Amazon.com marketplace. I couldn't get through the hundred year-old system of traditional publishing, but Amazon.com offered me this completely new way of reaching my readers with my books. In return, they take most of the proceeds, but making my "product" available in their marketplace is very much worth it to me. They help me sell my books by introducing them to a market I could never reach on my own.

Too good to be true

Before the Great Recession[12], people could publish a half-decent website and expect results. For many small businesses, it was easy enough to scoop up at least some sales from their new website. Competition wasn't too tough and customers had money to spend.

So what happened? First of all, the Great Recession which began in late 2008 caused a sharp decline in many companies' traditional revenue sources. The promise of sales over the Internet looked like a relatively cheap way of covering the shortfall in revenue, so many of these companies started a project to build their first real Internet presence. They hired consultants, went to seminars, read books and searched the Internet for clues about how to make a go of this new opportunity. I call these companies *Bricks-and-Mortar Refugees,* whose hunger for revenue drove them to the Internet in search of satisfaction.

Some of us were living on the Internet in one way or another before these refugees began to show up. Business was easy, and success was often a question of putting up a solid website and doing some basic SEO[13] work to help buyers find your site and make purchases.

---

12 For convenience, I'll call the recession that started at the end of 2008 The Great Recession.
13 SEO: Search Engine Optimization: the art and science of helping search engines find you and list you high up in their search results when folks go looking for what you provide.

Not so today.

By early 2010, I was hearing and seeing something different from prospects and businesses across the land. I was hearing that they *used* to appear at the top of search results, but lately, were falling to the second, third, fourth page, or not appearing at all in search results. *Has Google changed its algorithms?* they would ask me. At first glance, it seemed that Google had indeed changed its algorithms, which decide who appears at the top of search results. Indeed, search engines are always refining how they decide which web pages display first in search results. However, after some investigation, I saw that something else was going on.

I examined these new websites that did appear at the top of search results, and found that the criteria for top placement had not changed in any meaningful way. Rather, *more companies were doing more of the right things* to get noticed by search engines, and were consequently pushing the sleepy incumbents off the top of the list of search results.

It must have been like that in the early twentieth century for Olympic competitors. One by one, every sport would become the focus of professionals. As the decades passed, science and human power were explored and studied. Every possible angle was exploited in the hopes of winning a medal at the Olympics, making it progressively more competitive as the years passed.

Today, companies realize they must take their web presence seriously and that to survive, they need an effective Internet presence, even if their revenue in the short term comes from word-of-mouth or other traditional channels and marketplaces.

Gone are the times when you could get your nephew to build your website on the cheap or, God help us, build it yourself. We live in a time when a sharp, professionally built website is only the starting point to business survival. Today, almost every small business needs Twitter, Facebook, an active blog and an integrated prospect management system, all woven together to form what is called an *Internet Presence*.

To summarize what we have covered so far, the ingredients of a profitable Internet Presence are:

1. A market must exist for what you sell.
2. New, relevant content is added to your website regularly.
3. Good SEO practices are applied.
4. Time.

Developing a web presence is like growing a forest. There's lots of planting involved, and patience is required, but most of all, it is the daily planting, care and attention early on that reward you with a profitable business in the long term. That is, once your web presence reaches critical mass.

Short term vs. long term

About twice a week, I get a phone call from a stranger – a different stranger each time, I mean – asking me to join with them on a sure-fire way of making lots of money on the Internet. Their plan is usually this: *I* would use my SEO and marketing expertise and *they* would provide the seed idea and business development.

It's usually a short conversation.

> *In business, there's no such thing as a good short term decision*

I've tried all manner of experiments on the Internet, and the only ones that worked were those with a long term focus. Sure, we've all heard stories of folks who made it big on the Internet, but building your business plan based on anecdotes or exceptions is always a bad idea. My experience has been that short term success plans fail in the long term. It is because, when more people compete for short term successes, the odds against success are more like the odds of winning the lottery. There are many other reasons why making decisions based on the long term is always better. The one I like most is, long term dedication to your any business project produces a qualitatively superior result. The longer you focus on building and refining an idea, the deeper and more comprehensively it is likely to address a problem and thus, more likely to be successful and profitable. I might even go so far as to say that *anything of value takes about ten years to create*. Certainly, my own experience tells me, *it takes a new business three years to discover its success formula*. And that is just the beginning.

It takes a new business about three years to discover its success formula

So, make your decisions with the future – measured in years – in mind. There really are no good short term decisions. Whether it's a new hire, a website or a marketing plan, every step should be taken with the longest term horizon possible in mind. If you think there is a "quick buck" to be made along the way, you will see that it is a false economy in the long term or at the very least, adds nothing to the value of your long term business.

That's not to say you can't make good money on short term deals or opportunities. Not everything has to pay off in the long term. It is just that, the core value of a real company is measured in years.

As you make decisions for the web presence for your small company, always think about how even the smallest of these decisions takes you closer to your *ten year vision*. If you can't see how it contributes to that, there should be a darn good reason why.

You are a Bricks-and-Mortar Refugee in the New Land of the Internet. It will take time for you to establish your presence. Your new website is the *foundation of a new marketplace*, and it takes time to grow a new marketplace from scratch.

The big are swallowing the small

For all the reasons listed above, it is a higher stakes game today than it was a few years ago – in money and in effort – to get a business to appear at the top of search results. On average, the rewards have not increased at the same rate as the cost has. The Great Recession is responsible for that too, as budgets are tightened and shoppers ask you to deliver more value for less money. This has resulted in smaller companies being forced to either end their business on the Internet or join forces with similar businesses in order to – roughly speaking – share the cost of surviving in the marketplace.

Let me explain this phenomenon with an example. Back in 2007, a stay-at-home mom – let's call her Mary – makes necklaces by hand and sells them through her website. Two years earlier, she paid someone $500 to develop the simple website for her tiny business. Up until 2008, she was making about twenty dollars profit per necklace. She sold one or two a day, and each customer found her through a search engine. In 2008, the Great Recession hit, and although traffic to her website stayed the same, her sales dropped by about 80% because people were now more reluctant to spend their money. As if that weren't bad enough, about a year later, traffic through her website dropped to nothing, causing her already paltry sales to dry up completely. A little investigation showed that her website now appeared, for the same search that brought her to the top three months earlier, on page *seven* – and sometimes not at all – of search results.

Mary has two compounding problems. First, the Recession hit the market for her products, shrinking it to a fraction of the size. Second, the Recession sent a wave of hungry new competitors into her market, taking what was left. It was like a *tsunami* wiped out what was left after the earthquake that caused it hit.

It truly must have felt like it did for those gold prospectors who were making a modest income panning for gold before they were overrun by thousands of crazed newcomers when the Gold Rush of California began in 1848.

Newcomers can still make money on the Internet – every year sees a substantial increase of web sales globally and nationally – it's just gotten harder to generate revenue with a tiny new website.

Recap: Questions to ask yourself

1. The very first question you must answer is: *Is there a market for what you are selling?*
    You might laugh at such an obvious question, but many people don't understand fully what "a market exists" means. It is necessary to understand this core requirement well, because if a market does not exist, you will not be successful. At the very least, without a market, your ambitions on the Internet are a long shot, because the implication is you have to *create* your market.
    It takes a large company to create a market. The likes of Apple and Microsoft come to mind.
    Getting back to what "a market exists" means: A market exists if *people are spending money today solving the problem you solve*. It doesn't matter how cool your product sounds, or what problem it solves. People have to be spending money to make your product a success.
    When people are *already spending money* on a solution like yours, if they ever find you, you only have to convince them that *yours* is the best solution

available in the market, not that they have a problem to begin with.

2. The second question I ask a potential client is, *Do you have any profitable customers*?
Until you've sold some of your own product – and the customers are satisfied and profitable – you don't know how far you are away from having a viable business. Your product could indeed be finished and ready to go, or it could be so flawed, you need to start over. You can proceed with your plans on the Internet without the achievement of profitable customers, but it may turn out to be an expensive way to learn your product is not market-ready, or that you don't know how to sell it. Or both.

3. The third question is, *Do you have the resources (time, money, patience) to develop a brand (on the Internet)?*
You might get lucky, but you can't plan on it. The list of overnight success stories on the Internet is short – I can't even think of one right now – so you have to be prepared to type a lot of blog postings, answer a lot of questions, and tweet like a starling, perhaps for more than a year, before you see the first fruits of your efforts.
Yes, there are ways to stuff leads into your sales funnel by advertising like crazy or buying access to email lists, and so on, but it is an expensive way to acquire leads. If the average new customer brought you fifty dollars profit, and you needed one hundred leads for every customer gained, you'd have to get each lead for fifty cents just to break even.

Developing your brand loyalty – in this New Age of the Internet – involves a lot of typing of blog postings, Twitter postings, answers to questions in online forums and other areas. The payoff is excellent, but it takes time, and many business owners don't have the resources to last that long. Prospects come to me with the expectation that they will be living off the proceeds within six months of starting their new website business. That would be spectacular, of course, if it were to happen, but it is a rare occurrence.

A metaphor I use for the path to success on the Internet is that of growing a forest; you do a lot of planting, pruning and feeding, but most of all, the project needs *time*. Time for all of your efforts to grow, connect and eventually, take on a life of their own. The better the sapling, the better the tree, the better the forest. The more you plant, the bigger your forest will be. Expect to spend a year planting saplings every day before you see the first fruits. And plan for another six to twelve months beyond that before you make decent money and know the business you are in. OK, enough of the forest metaphors, I promise!

4. *What is your core competency?*
   You could ask this question of anyone going into business. What are you good at? No matter what business you are in, you really need to know your stuff, because you will have competitors that know theirs. The harder the subject matter is, the better off you are, if you are an expert at it.
   This is another seemingly obvious question, but you

would be surprised at how many people meet me with an Internet business idea of which their (or their team's) skill is not an ingredient. Many such business plans are simply putting three or four things together and hoping the sum exceeds the whole. It won't. If it did, you'd be overwhelmed with competition as soon as you opened for business.

For example, *let's get someone to build a website, we'll sign up for a bunch of affiliate programs, add a bunch of products and collect the cash when lots of visitors buy the products*. Such a plan would be crushed by a competitor with deep expertise in Affiliate Marketing, for example, or Search Engine Optimization, or both.

You can pay someone to build you a great website, write your blog postings, tweet your tweets and do a bunch of marketing for you, but you must bring your own hard skill to the mix. It might be that you an experienced oncologist who can provide expert product support to your cancer treatment equipment sales team. You could be an experienced HVAC (Heating, Ventilation, Air Conditioning) plumber giving advice on your HVAC forum. Perhaps you are a high-end lighting equipment salesperson who can advise prospective designers – prospects visiting your website – on how best to use the products you sell.

Whatever business you bring to the Internet, the more expertise you inject into it, the better your chances of success.

What does a complete web presence look like?

A typical web presence looks like this:

"A *website built using a Content Management System, a Twitter and Facebook account linked to it, and a blog built into it. The website contains a few videos to help visitors understand what you do. A professional brand/logo. New website content is published every day with tweets and/or Facebook postings to support it. By way of one or more Target Landing Pages, visitors are converted into leads.*"

That's it in a nutshell. Of course, each organization's web presence is different. Some won't use Twitter, others will rely on it heavily.

Let's talk about the foundation of your web presence: your website.

Chapter 2 - Your new website

How much will it cost?

How much does a website cost? "How long is a piece of string?", is how my father would answer the question with another question.

The cost of a website varies from *Almost Free* to *Millions of Dollars*. At the cheap end of the spectrum you can sign up with GoDaddy.com (or one of countless other hosting companies) and be up and running on your new website in an hour. It might cost about fifty dollars, and it will look every bit if it. And that might be enough for you. Some businesses need a vanilla website to reflect the modest means of the visitors they are seeking, so a "fifty-buck website" might well be enough.

On the other end of the spectrum, IBM or Apple or other high tech company may spend millions of dollars each year on their respective website. It all depends on what a given business is trying to do.

In my own business, Siteleads.net, I provide website building services with a heavy focus on SEO[14] for small to medium-sized companies. Prices range from about $10,000 to about $100,000. Occasionally, I get the opportunity to build something beyond the scope of what I can reasonably handle on my own with a couple of assistants, so I refer the opportunity to a larger web development company. Beyond

---

14 SEO – Search Engine Optimization – work performed to make a website appear in the non-advertising area towards the top of search results, when people search for your type of solution on the Internet.

a certain point, a substantial team is required to finish the job, so I will pass it to a company that has such resources.

There is another well serviced market of website development in the "above $50 and below $10,000" range. Many small companies have limited means and modest ambitions on the web, so getting a small company to develop a $2,000 website can often be enough.

If you are a plumber, your website might be a few pages. You might have a *Testimonials* page, a *Services* page and a *Contact Us* page, without a "shopping basket" or fancy graphics. In fact, you might *want* it to look plain. In some industries or professions, an expensive looking website can scare people away by sending the message "we are expensive". A plumber's website might do better with a down-to-earth look, giving prospects the idea that his or her prices are also down-to-earth. A medical equipment manufacturer, however, may not want to give that impression on their website.

The cost of making your new website public is just the beginning, and a lot depends on what you are trying to achieve. There is a correlation between the profit potential of typical products and services in your market and the price you might expect to pay for your website. If you make $20 jewelry pieces on your kitchen table, your profit margins are so small, your website budget might be $500 or less, but your competition will have similar constraints, so an inexpensive website might be perfectly fine. If you sell $400,000 pieces of medical equipment, your supporting website may cost tens of thousands of dollars or more.

Bricks to Clicks

When I am talking to a new prospect for the very first time, I try to set expectations as early as possible by talking about how much their website is probably going to cost – at least – if they ask me to develop it for them. After they recover from the initial shock, we talk about why is has to cost ten thousand dollars – or thirty thousand dollars – or whatever price range I ballpark at this early stage. Many prospects are confused by the range of price quotes they receive from different vendors, so I use an analogy of buying a new car. Even on a single car sales lot, a brand new four-door automobile can cost $13,000 while another might cost $67,000. What is the difference? One is a Toyota Yaris an the other is a Toyota Land Cruiser. They are both new cars, and each of them will take you across town, but clearly, they are different. For some lucky folks, writing a check for $67,000 doesn't cost them a second thought, while others struggle with the purchase of a $13,000 car. It is the same in business. There is an appropriate level of expenditure – and an equivalent required value – a business can expect to pay for and receive from their website.

And so, it all depends on what you are trying to achieve. One of my clients is a plastic surgeon whose average client profitability is over ten thousand dollars. Another client of mine sells weight-loss products with an average profit of about five dollars. The plastic surgeon only has to scoop up a handful of new clients to cover the cost of a $50,000 website, while the weight-loss company needs to close a thousand new customers to cover the cost of a $5,000 website.

There are so many variables, but here are price ranges for typical businesses:

- If you are a "mom-and-pop" store that doesn't expect to generate any new business from the Internet: $50 – 1,000.

- For a business that generates more than $50,000 profit a year: $1,000 - $5,000.

- Annual profit between $100k and $500k: $5,000 - $50,000

And then, there is the question of just how much new business is available to you on the Internet. It may indeed be too late to expect a good return on your website investment. Perhaps an established player has locked up your market with a commanding web presence and is selling the exact same products you are selling. On the other hand, a marketing professional might tell you that this actually presents an opportunity for you, because you absolutely know the market for your products exists.
So you see, there are many variables that affect likely costs of your new website.

Do I even need a website?

If you asked me back in 2007 if your business needed a website, I might have answered with a *Most Likely, Yes.*

Times have changed.

The increase in competition for the top position in search results has made it more expensive – in time and money – to get your website to appear there. Only those organizations who make the investment get those top slots. This increase in competition has spawned a new kind of website – a "directory" website – which offers a position in their online directory to those companies who cannot afford to appear on page one of search results under their own steam. So, instead of the *Acme Law Firm of Lower Manhattan* appearing on the first page of search results, a Directory of law firms appears as if it were a single company. That directory might contain hundreds of law firms around the country, but depending on what search the person entered, a different page of the directory is displayed.

Such Directories invest a lot more than any one company can invest on its own, and they ask for a fee from each small company in order to be included in the directory. This is best explained with an example:

Joe is a maintenance guy for a building in Lower Manhattan. He's got a leaking faucet, so he needs a plumber. In Google, he searches for the words "Plumber Lower Manhattan". He doesn't see any actual plumbing company websites, but he sees ServiceMagic (a company that offers different types of services) and a national plumbing directory. He clicks the latter and is taken to a page that shows a local plumbing company. It's not the plumbing company's actual website, but a page in the directory with all the details Joe needs to get the help he needs.

In addition to such "directory" companies, Google and other search engines often display a list of local businesses – up to ten of them together on the first page of search results – which you can follow by clicking any of their respective links. This is called *Google Places*, and to make your business appear there, you use Google Maps. That is explained in *Google Places* on page 87. It's easy, free and a business doesn't even need a website to get listed there.

If your target market is local, then it will be worth your while getting your company to appear in Google Places.

What should my new website look like?

Big question.

For so many companies today, their website offers the very first impression potential customers will get of them. So, you'd think it would be of paramount importance. Still, many companies decide to skimp on this strategic element of their business, delegating the task to an outsider or throwing together a fifty-dollar website that looks like it cost, well, fifty dollars.

Doing it the hard way

Sometimes I must do something the wrong way several times before the correct – and obvious – way dawns on me.

And so it was when I backed into this business of developing websites for small companies. I knew a lot about SEO, but more and more, my clients were asking me to also develop their entire web presence, including the website itself. I'd start the design and development process as a single task, designing and developing as I went. Soon, I had something to show my client. The problem was, it wasn't what they wanted. Armed with a bit of feedback, I'd dive right back into the process for another week or more, returning again to the client to show him progress. Still, it wasn't what he wanted, so after three or four frustrating iterations of this, I took him on a visit to the Internet. We would go, shoulder-to-shoulder, looking for a website that he liked, with a view to copying it.

It took two or three sessions of about two or three hours each to find a website that my client really liked. The process involved searching for a similar business in another town – perhaps a city where my client did not expect to do business, so no competitive issues would arise – and come up with a list of about twenty websites, one of which would become the "Base Website" design. In addition, we'd have a list of design exceptions. For example, "make the navigation bar dark gray instead of light gray" or "move the search button to the bottom of the right hand column", "add our 1-800 number to the top banner", and so on.

Sometimes, my client wouldn't be able to decide right away, but needed – very understandably – lots more time to browse the 'net before coming up with that initial list of potential websites to base our initial design on.

Drawing my client into the website design process in this fashion has a profound effect on the success likelihood of the project. There are four reasons for this. 1. From the beginning, my client is taking significant ownership in the outcome of his or her own website, 2. Before development starts, everyone knows what the website is supposed to look like, 3. It is easy to predict when the website will be delivered and 4. Development and delivery of the website only has to occur once.

There are plenty of challenges, technical and otherwise, but delivering the website to the satisfaction of my client is the foundation of everything that is to follow.

Since I adopted this methodology – and I adhere to it strictly now – every new client I serve is very satisfied with the result.

So, let's go over this process step-by-step. I call it the *success formula for developing a website*. Whether you are a small business owner or a website developer wanting the very best result for your client, this success formula won't let you down.

Deciding on your website appearance – the "success formula"

1. Search the Internet for websites that may become the base look-and-feel of your new website. If you can, come up with a dozen or so candidates. Search for businesses like your client's, but in other towns. For example, if you are developing a website for a resort spa in Southern California, search for similar businesses in Florida, Hawaii, other overseas locations or on other continents. You will soon find other businesses that have put a lot of thought into developing a website that "speaks to their customers". Cherry-picking ideas from all of them can save you a lot of time and money. Take as much time as needed for this part, pulling in other team members who might have a contribution to make. The more people with "skin in the game", the more people will own the result.

2. Narrow the list down to three, to two, then one base website. Again, sitting down at a table with the entire website development team will ensure every

player will not only make a contribution but is more likely to support the project to the end.

3. Make out a detailed list of all the specific changes you wish to make to that base design. Remember there will be differences in the design of the Home Page of the website to Product Pages or Service pages, and so on. Make the list as detailed as you can. Include everything you think of, however small the detail may sound. If a change is big enough to see on a screen, add it to your list.

4. Gather up screen shots and notes from everything you've produced so far. Together, they make up the beginnings of your website development plan.

5. Add notes on what you want the website to do. For example, "allow visitors to use their credit card to buy products", "allow tax to be calculated differently per state", "I want a rotating set of client testimonials on the front page", or "can I collect visitor contact details from the special offer page?" and so on. A lot of these ideas may come from other websites you have seen, as well as what you know the website needs to do for your exact business. It all helps.

You can actually get this far into the project on your own, without any technical assistance and without spending money, pasting all your screen shots and typed notes into a simple word processing document. If you've been rigorous about it, you already have a far better website development plan than 90% of those I've seen developed by companies who do this for a living.

You will find the first step – making a shortlist of website candidates – is quite a difficult undertaking. It is the process of answering the question *What do you want to look like*? I have found that my clients struggle with that quite a lot and many tell me later that it was the most challenging part of the project for them. Just think about that for a moment. If you struggled trying to decide what your own website should look like, imagine how difficult it must be for an outsider to do it.

When will my website appear on page one of search results?

If your customers are "within driving distance" of your business, it is likely to be much easier for you to appear at the top of search results than if your customers are far away. The reason is, if all of your competition is close by, then there is a manageable limit to the number of competitors you can possibly have. If your business is a home-delivery pizza joint in my home town of Bellevue, Washington, you might have a dozen competitors. You won't have competition from the suburbs of Chicago, or even Seattle, which is on the other side of a lake, putting them out of your reach and into someone else's market.

A home delivery pizza business would be about as close to its customers as it gets simply because pizza goes cold and the profit margins are low; every mile further away adds real cost to the pizza, limiting the business' geographic reach to within a few miles probably. As your potential customer base widens geographically, so too does the number of competitors you face increase, along with the effort required to appear at the top of search results.

If you are selling hand-made necklaces and hoping to reach a nationwide market, you are competing with everyone in the country who has a similar product to yours and has matching aspirations.

You might have a vastly superior product, the best looking website on Earth and the most attractive prices on the Internet, but it won't help if you don't appear on Page One of search results. At least, not as far as search is concerned. It's understandable then that companies expend so much effort in appearing there. The promise of selling product at a national level, and grabbing the lion's share of the market brings out the greed in the best of us.

Common mistakes in SEO

1. **Not including keywords in page titles**
   You might be surprised at how many websites make this mistake. Hopefully your competitors do, because it reduces their search engine attractiveness substantially. Possibly the single most important factor in a web page's ability to match search words is this page title.
   It's like the title of a resumé. No matter what is below it, a resumé's title is the first gating factor for whether a candidate has a chance of being considered for employment. Imagine how far your resume would get if it had "Welcome to my resume" at the top of it! That's what a lot of people do to their website: whatever program they used to

build their website, set a default title for each page. "Welcome to Acme Products Inc" doesn't help search engines match search words with a page that has that in its title, but "bicycle rentals and repairs in Lower Manhattan" tells search engines a lot about what might be on the page.

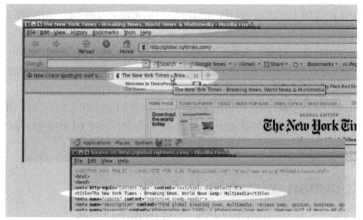

Illustration 3: The page title appears in the top bar of your browser and the page tab, and comes from the <title> tag of the page.

2. **Having the same page title on every page of your website**

Like mistake number 1, above, many websites use the same keywords in the page title of every page of their website.

Consider each page of your website to be a kind of lottery ticket; each one is another opportunity for search engines to match your website against a specific search someone is requesting. "bicycle rentals and repairs in Lower Manhattan" looks like a good page title, but not if it is the same on every page of your website. Variations might include: "bike rentals and servicing in New York" or "rent your bike at Manhattan, New York" and so on. Each page title should be a variation of a given set of likely search words.

You've probably seen the situation where multiple pages from the same website appear at the top of search results. This happens when multiple pages on a single website match the search words for different reasons.

3. **Not adding content every day**

With a bit of effort, most organizations can get a website built. If they can't actually built it themselves, a few phone calls and Internet searches is usually enough to get hold of the right person or company to do the job. Website *content*, on the other hand, is a lot more challenging. In particular, website content that attracts visitors through search engines is difficult to create consistently. The main challenge is to find someone who can write quality material that is germane to your business, and to keep doing it over a long period of time.

Page 161 talks about adding content every day, how it's done and how to keep doing it.

When a website does not get at least one new page added to it every day, it tends to fall quickly from the top of search results, no matter how fine or search engine optimized the content on your website is.

Should I invest in a mass email campaign?

A few years ago, you could buy access to millions of email addresses in the hope of converting a percentage of them to customers. You'd provide a company with your target demographics (e.g. male, married, income > $50k, sports enthusiast) and a "sales email" would be sent out to each of them. A percentage of the recipients would open the email, a percentage of *those* would click and visit your site, and a *fraction* of those would give you their contact details, at which point you might begin the sales process. The math was simple: if the profit at the end of the cycle was greater than the cost of the campaign, you could repeat the process with another million emails, and so on.

Unfortunately, a number of recent developments have made this model far less likely to succeed. Firstly, Gmail, Yahoo, Hotmail, MSN and other email systems have gotten a lot better at filtering out spam[15] messages, because their users didn't want to be spammed, not even about subjects they were interested in. This type of traditional in-your-face marketing campaign fits in the category of "Outbound Marketing". We continue to move from an "Outbound Marketing" model to an "Inbound Marketing" model, and the effectiveness of email mass marketing campaigns is one of the casualties. The moral of the story? Don't waste your money on mass email marketing campaigns.

---

15 Spam: unwanted marketing or sales promotion emails arriving in
    your email inbox.

How to make your business appear in local searches

As described earlier, your market is *local* if your customers are, roughly speaking, within driving distance of you.

Google, Microsoft and other search engine providers each have a way for a business to tell the search engines where their business is physically located. You have probably seen the result of it already. Use Google or Bing to search for "pizza home delivery" and you will see a list of local businesses displayed in a slightly different way to how search results are usually displayed. Sometimes a link to a map location is given. These search results are selected by search engines in a different way than normal search results and can be a very powerful lead generator for those whose customers live within a few miles of the business.

In the last eight months, both of these search engines have significantly changed the way businesses add their locations several times. So rather than provide you with specific steps that will be out of date before the ink dries, I will point you to Google's and Microsoft's own instructions of how to add your business to their respective local search databases.

How to add your business to Google Places:

Http://www.google.com/support/places or search for "Google Places".

How to add your business to Microsoft Bing:

http://www.bing.com/businessportal

Both in Google Places and in Microsoft Bing, there are two fields that have a significant influence on whether you appear in that first page of local listings. They are *Business name* and *Description*. For example, a business name of *Acme Plumbing Company* is less likely to appear in a local search listing than the business name *Acme Plumbing of Lower Manhattan*. It is the same with Business Description. Make sure it includes plenty of references to your location. For example: *Plumbing, gas piping and sewer installation, repair and maintenance services in the King County, Redmond, Bellevue, Issaquah and Sammamish areas*. Include your best keywords (*plumbing, gas piping, sewer, repair,* etc.) with your best locations. When someone does a search for "*plumbing repair issaquah*" your company name and description provide a match for it, even if your business is physically located in an adjacent city.

There are books upon books written on each of these two services, and I would need hundreds of pages to explain either of them. Fortunately, both Google and Microsoft have gone out of their way to make it pretty straightforward. And if you make sure your business name and description are written as I described in the previous paragraph, it might be all you ever need to generate more local leads.

The top of search results is not everything

So your competitors have spent a small fortune forcing their way to the top of search results. Between a few of them, they have totally crowded you out from Page One and it seems you'll never get there. What is there left to do?

Lots.

Blog like crazy

(For more detail on writing effective blog postings see the section on page 34).

One of the biggest factors in appearing at the top of search results is the number of Inbound Links (sometimes called *backlinks*) to your website. An Inbound Link is something on a page of *someone else's website* that, when clicked, takes the person to a page on *your* website.

I occasionally post an article to the Bank of America Small Business Forum, and at the bottom of each article, I include a link back to my website (perhaps to a page that describes one of my books). Every time I do that, I get a spike in visitors to my website, and a small temporary increase in book sales sometimes occurs. Three phenomena occur when you create such an Inbound Link to your site: (1) some people simply click the link to visit your website, (2) search engines add that link to your website's total count of Inbound Links, increasing your website's value in their eyes and (3) the keywords and other content on the website with the link strengthen the value of those same words on *your* website.

An Inbound Link to your website is what is called *Off Page* SEO, because it is something that helps your website traffic but does not live on your website.

Writing a top notch article takes a bit of work, of course. You only have to watch your teenage son trying to write a short essay on the American Revolution to understand how tortuous it can be. There's a way to make it easier, though.

Instead of spending hours writing a single article on someone else's website, write a much shorter article on your own website. Let's say you're a financial advisor, and you've just read about a new law that raises taxes on early 401k withdrawals. You post a two-sentence commentary of it to your own blog on your own website, then you point to it via a short Tweet on your Twitter account, Facebook and perhaps one or two external forums (like the Bank of America one I mentioned earlier). Your Tweet might be "How to reduce your tax burden despite the new law:" followed by the link to your blog posting. If the posting is perceived as valuable, you might get a few re-tweets, which will add yet more links to your website. And so, your small daily efforts begin to pay off.

Brush your teeth, post to your blog

If you have more time than money, making such a blog posting every night while you're watching TV is a great way of steadily increasing the value of your website. For most of us, writing every night is drudgery, especially after a hard day's work, but for a small business needing to make it on the Internet on a shoestring budget, it is as important as brushing your teeth is to your dental health. Promise yourself you'll write a blog posting right after you brush your teeth, every time, and I'll promise you you'll have a high value, well-trafficked website in twelve months.

Just imagine. If you make two postings per day, and each of them resulted in two Inbound Links (created by readers of your blog postings), your website would have over a thousand Inbound Links in less than a year. That's a lot for almost any small business. Use WebsiteGrader.com to count the number of Inbound Links each of your competitors has.

Making it interesting

Most people use Twitter and Facebook to distribute the most boring details of their mundane lives to an equally bored audience. I've seen grown men post to Facebook about what they plan to have for dinner. "I'm having liver and onions for dinner this evening. I paid $2.95/lb for the liver at the Kingston Safeway. Wish me luck!" Later that evening, they post a photo of the half eaten repast with a comment like "it was delicious! Bet you wish you were me!" and so on.
Torture.

Nobody – except maybe my mother – cares what I ate for dinner. If you want to use Twitter and Facebook to grow your business, post *valuable* information. Instead of telling the world what you plan to have for dinner, give them a valuable fact you have learned in your business. Likely, your followers will be interested in your *business*, which is why they are following you. Reward them with valuable nuggets of your hard-earned wisdom. They will tell their friends about you, and others will find you and follow you because your valuable postings will find their way to more and more people.

You might even offer a product for free on occasion. One of my clients offers a free, 300-page eBook on how to improve your golf swing. In return, his website asks for the visitor's contact information. As time passes, his contact list grows, and he stays in regular contact with all of them, delivering with each conversation another piece of golfing magic he learned over forty years of being a golfing instructor. He adds subtle and very targeted ads in his communications with this prospect base and a percentage of them buy products from him as a result.

Chapter 3 - The three stages of closing business on the web

You have made the big decision. You have committed to developing your web presence on the Internet. At a very high level, you have to drive strangers to your website, take control of the conversation with them when they arrive and sell them something later. Each stage requires a distinctly different skill set, and each has to be done right for it to result in a sale.

Stage 1: Attract

This is mostly what is called Search Engine Optimization. You want strangers to find your website – those strangers who are looking for a solution like yours. I won't talk about paid advertising here (because it frightens the life out of me) and focus on how you are going to get your website to appear at the top of search results for free. That is, when someone who never heard of you searches for a solution like yours, they see your sweet website appear on the list Google gives them. It's that simple and it's that hard. It's simple because you know exactly what you want and it's hard because you will likely have to do some real work to make it happen.

I won't try to cram every piece of technical SEO skill I have into this one paragraph, but I do want you to walk away with a clear understanding of the nature of the work and where it will fit into your Internet Marketing Plan.

Driving strangers to your website – without using advertising – is achieved by making changes to your website and by adding things to other organizations' websites.

Fixing your website

Before we dive into what is to be fixed, let's see what's broken.

Does your business already have a website? If it does, however humble you might think it is, you can give it a free health check right now, if you have a connection to the Internet. To do it, visit the website www.WebsiteGrader.com. It is a useful, free service provided by the good folks at HubSpot and it will show you how your website stacks up against millions of other websites. You simply type in your own website URL[16] (without the usual "http://", e.g. www.myfancywebsite.com) and click the orange button. A few moments later, it will provide you with a percentile score achieved by *your* website versus millions of others it has examined, and it provides you with a list of things you can repair to make your website more visible to search engines.

The good thing about WebsiteGrader.com is that it delivers a *percentile* score, so you can measure how your website is doing *relative* to your competitors, along a spectrum of millions of websites out there. The higher your score relative to your competitors, the more likely it is you will appear ahead of them in search results. Still, the tool

---

16 URL stands for "Uniform Resource Locater". It means Internet Address and is often pronounced "Earl".

doesn't tell you if your keywords are all messed up – and we'll talk about how to fix that later – but it does give you a measure of how *architecturally* suitable your website is for search engines to find what they need. I've found WebsiteGrader.com to be an accurate predictor of success when it comes to appearing in search results.

If your competitors score in the range of 70-80%, aim for over 90%. In fact, no matter what your competitors' scores are, you need to beat them substantially on the WebsiteGrader scale to know you have a chance of appearing before them in search results. You don't have to beat their score to see the first results of your efforts, though. You just have to get close to their score before you start stealing a sliver of their traffic by appearing a tiny percentage of the time ahead them in search results.

Don't panic if you see your competitors' with a score you feel you can't reach. The score is important, but another important factor – which WebsiteGrader can't possibly measure – is how well you have selected and placed your keywords, and how fresh your website content is. And there is lots more we can do, too.

The Most Important Factors

In order of importance, here is a list of things on your website you need to get right. I won't go into technical detail of how to fix each, because a lot depends on the tool you use to manage content on your website, but at least, you'll get what you need to ask the right questions – and make the right requests – of whoever is managing your website today. Remember, if you find something a bit vague, or want more detail, or simply have any question about this, I will personally answer your question on the website www.sboseries.com. I do want to hear from you. I touch on some of these points elsewhere in the book, but this list is something you can pass to your webmaster:

1. Every page on your website should have a title. You'd be surprised at how many websites leave the page title blank. The page title is perhaps the single most important factor in what gets placed at the top of search results.

2. Any image you place on your website should be named using likely search words that you want to match to the page. a*luminum-ten-speed-bicycle.jpg* is a more search engine-friendly file name than *image500a.jpg*. Search engines use these image names to determine what the page is likely to contain.

3. Every image you place on your website should have an "alternate text" (or "alt text") associated with it. This reinforces the page's ownership of keywords. The alt text *"visit our aluminum racing bicycle store in kirkland, wa, 98033"* is superior to no alt text.

4. Every image on your website should have a title containing keywords. Image title is different from image name or image alt text.

5. Use a Content Management System (WordPress, Joomla, Drupal, ExpressionEngine and Big Medium are good examples) to manage the content of your website. They generally produce pages that are more transparent to search engines and are thus

more likely to reach the top of search results. They also allow you to manage the content of your website in a more disciplined and productive way.

Stage 2: Engage

You've done a lot of work to attract visitors to your website and at long last, you're beginning to see some traffic. How do you count the arrivals, what they do when they get there, and how do you turn them into good old-fashioned leads?

Measuring Arriving Visitors

There is an indispensable (and free – I love that bit) tool out there that can easily be installed into your website that gives you powerful insights into a lot of things that happen on your website. The tool is called Google Analytics and it gives you insights into just about everything that happens on your website, for example:

- How many unique visitors per day
- How many visitors leave after visiting only one page (the "bounce rate")
- Which search engines sent how many visitors
- What search words did visitors use to find your website
- Which pages did they visit

And so on.

I listed just five pieces of information. There is a whole lot more, but those five are my favorite. If you ran a paid ad campaign, you could send responders to a hidden page on

your website, then use Google Analytics to tell you exactly
how many folks clicked the ad. That's a very simple
example. There is more in there to help you than I could
cover in five hundred pages. Illustration 4 on page 98
shows a report indicating how many visitors arrived from
search engines. A very valuable piece of information!

Can strangers see activity reports for my website?

No one can see Google Analytics reports for your website
unless you explicitly let them. Many people ask me that
question the moment they see just how powerful these
reports are.

*Illustration 4: Google Analytics
showing (highlighted) origins of website
traffic*

One of the most telling pieces of information that comes
from Google Analytics is what is called the "bounce rate".
The Bounce Rate is the percentage of arriving visitors that

leave your site before ever looking at a page beyond the page they arrived at. So, if you had a bounce rate of 75% of visitors coming from an ad you placed on the Internet, you might need to improve the page the ad sent them to if you consider a 75% bounce rate to be too high. There is more information on bounce rate on page 41.

The Engage Stage involves capturing the contact information of visitors so that you can develop a relationship with them. But there is a catch. Obviously people are reluctant to give their email address to just any old website, so you need to offer them something in exchange. Sometimes it is enough just to offer them a subscription to your newsletter, but often, you have to give them something a little more valuable. One of my clients offers one of his eight products for free in exchange for the visitor's basic contact information. Mind you, his products are digital (golf training media), so the cost of giving one away is low. As you have probably learned in your business already, quality sales leads can be expensive, so giving something away for free can be a lot cheaper than traditional methods of sales lead generation, like trade shows or advertising. Still, only you can know what it is that attracts people in your market.

Capturing Contact Information

By now, you're getting your first trickle of website traffic from search engines and you've decided on what you want to give away to your prospects in exchange for their contact information. The next thing you need is a few input boxes on your web page that the visitor must fill out and submit. Fortunately, this has gotten a lot easier than it was even a few years ago. A number of fairly sophisticated online services do this for you. Starting from about ten dollars a month, any of several such contact management companies will give you a gadget to add to your website that allows visitors to enter their contact information. As the visitors do so, the contact management company stores that info in a database on their servers. Later, you can examine this database and decide to communicate with its members in a way that supports your sales and marketing efforts.

This is by no means an exhaustive list of online contact management solutions. There are dozens, maybe hundreds, of others out there:

1. iContact.com
2. ConstantContact.com
3. Aweber.com
4. AllClients.com

ConstantContact.com is one of the more popular, if I am to judge by the number of emails I get with their logo on the bottom of them. I've looked at all four, and at my own company we use iContact.com because it seemed the simplest to use at the time we signed up. They all had what looked like similar functionality, but by the time you read this, all that may have changed, so it is worth your while to examine these four and others to see which offers the best solution for your own organization's needs.

If budget is an issue, take a look at how many contacts you can store at what monthly price. Some solutions are better suited to the management of large numbers of sales leads, while others appear to focus on serving small companies.

Another solution you may explore is that of EmailMeForm.com which allows you to design pretty much any input form for your website, including support for image upload, but is not designed to support email/newsletter distribution to the contacts you have gathered.

At my company SiteLeads.net, we use EmailMeForm.com to gather any information other than contact details. For example, we use it to gather Trouble Ticket requests from our clients. It provides a number of options – like who gets notified – when a visitor has entered their issue and also supports secure data upload. EmailMeForm can do a lot, but you are better off using a contact management service, like any of the four listed above, to gather your visitors' information and to manage your communications with them while you work towards closing a sale.

Stage 3: Close

Very few small businesses manage to sell product to strangers directly from their website early on. For small, lower-priced items it is certainly easier, but for sales that run into the hundreds or thousands of dollars, visitors are usually unwilling to make a purchase on an unfamiliar website.

What has to be in place before a stranger buys directly from my website?

In a word, Brand. Your whole Internet strategy drives visitors to your website again and again, and as your content grows larger and larger – and you develop a relationship with a growing list of prospects – your brand begins to emerge in the minds of the buyers in your target market.

That simply takes time. Actually, it is a combination of money and time. If you have lots of cash to throw at the problem, you can reduce the time somewhat, but time is a powerful factor when you are making the right investments in all the important factors I cover in this book, like *content*, *backlinks*, *articles*, *new content* every day, and so on.

How can my website drive sales?

Even though sales will not come flooding into your spiffy new website immediately, there are ways to use your website to drive sales somewhere else, while buttressing the sale by referring prospects back to your website.

Imagine (again) you sell collectors quality military memorabilia on your website, but so far, visitors are reluctant to buy directly from you. They are nervous about buying from you because they've never heard of you or your store, even though your website is professionally designed and developed. So, you create a store on eBay, and name it using your existing business name. You sell some of your products there through eBay, each time adding a link back to your fancy new website. You are using eBay's brand – at a cost of course – to support building up your own brand over time. As you accumulate sales and references within the eBay marketplace, you can use that capital on your website using customer quotes and specific sales information (like sales revenue numbers or customer counts).

As your brand grows, your sales grow. Building your brand takes time. For at least a year, use your website early on to *generate leads*, not to sell products directly.

Bricks to Clicks

Chapter 4 - Content Management Systems (CMS)

Enter Content Management Systems

A Content Management System, or Web Content Management System, is a program that typically runs on the server hosting your website and allows one or more people to control the appearance, structure and content of the website.

There are hundreds of CMS programs on the market. Some website hosting companies[17] provide you with a CMS so you don't have to bother installing your own.

CMSs evolved to satisfy the need for tools to manage fast-changing, multiple-contributor websites protected by a robust login process.

Exit HTML Editors

Before CMSs, you had to build your website using a HTML Editor product. Examples of such programs are Dreamweaver, FrontPage, HomeSite and even simple text editors like Microsoft Notepad or the vi editor. You would construct your website on a PC then push[18] the whole thing up to a server where the whole world could see it. You can find a list of the more common HTML Editors on

---

17 Hosting Company: a company that stores your website on its servers and connects it to the Internet for you so you don't have to worry about it being available 24x7.

Wikipedia, or by simply doing an Internet search for *HTML Editors*.

> *Any organization that is serious about their web presence will use a Content Management System to manage their website and will not use a HTML Editor*

HTML Editors give you the ability to make changes and additions to your website directly. For example, if you needed to correct a spelling mistake on your home page, you would open up the home page text file, make the change, save it, then push the file back up to your website, overwriting the text file (your home page, actually) that contained the spelling mistake.

That direct access, while enabling you to make changes easily, resulted in an unacceptable level of risk to organizations that needed their website to be less prone to mistakes. It was so easy for the person changing the website to make a simple mistake and cause significant damage to the website. It was often hard to retrace ones steps in order to make corrections, and when more than one person was making changes, website maintenance and security could quickly spiral out of control.

The arrival of the CMS changed all that. A CMS doesn't allow the website contributors to access the website content directly. Instead, they must log in to a special page, and edit

---

18 "Pushing" website files up to a server usually involved an FTP program. FTP stands for File Transfer Protocol. There are hundreds of such FTP programs, which can be installed easily on a PC, available.

content from there. The CMS then updates the website contents based on what data was input by the person who logged in.

If you've ever added a comment to someone's website, or placed an order on Amazon.com, you've used a Content Management System. You typed in your comment and the CMS either published it immediately, or sent an email to the owner of the website to seek approval for the new comment before posting it to the website. All of the links back and forth within the website are managed by the CMS, and the comment you added to that website might actually result in a new page being created, in which case, a link to that new page would be automatically added from elsewhere on the site to the new page.

As I re-read that last paragraph, I do see that it sounds a bit complicated, but you don't have to know how it all works behind the scenes to take advantage of a CMS. A good CMS will expose you only to those pieces that are required for you to do your job, so if all you have to do is add a blog posting to your website every day, you just have to log in, type your blog posting and press the save button. The CMS will do everything else.

It's a bit like going to a restaurant. You read the menu, order your food, eat, pay and leave, without ever having to visit the kitchen or even worry about how the food is prepared. The food preparation (the "back end" work) is taken care of for you. The kitchen is kept stocked, cleaned and managed behind the scenes, so that you can focus directly on the purpose of your visit to the restaurant.

An online newspaper is an excellent example of a Content Management System at work. Dozens, sometimes hundreds or even thousands of contributors are adding content to the website, and it is all managed by a browser interface to the CMS. That interface, if I may continue the metaphor, represents the waiters in a restaurant.

Don't use a HTML Editor

The reasons for not using a HTML Editor (FrontPage, Dreamweaver, HomeSite, and so on) make for a long list. For example, they don't produce robust, object-oriented websites, don't offer the breadth and depth of features like scheduled publication, comments moderation, advanced security, easy multiple-contributor management and a thousand other powerful features.

What should a good content management system look like?

If you accept that you can't create a world class website without the use of a CMS, what then should a good CMS look like, what features should it have and what should you avoid?

Every website has different requirements, so you may well arrive at a different conclusion than I would for my own business. It all depends on what you are trying to achieve. In addition, if you plan only to create a single, simple website, and you don't have the time or background to get heavily involved in the technicalities, an easier – and potentially less powerful – CMS will make more sense than if you plan to make a living from website development.

You might compare it to the difference between assembling a set of Ikea bunk beds and becoming a professional carpenter. A professional carpenter will want to invest the time and money into the best set of tools available; his investment in education will pay him back over and over again as he produces a superb result time after time. The *Do-It-Yourselfer*, on the other hand, might spend five dollars on a single screwdriver to help him assemble the bunk beds, never to use the tool again.

In my own business, I might implement a dozen new websites a year. It pays me to understand Cascading Style Sheets, HTML, both browser- and server-based scripts of different types, Photoshop, and a host (no pun intended) of other tools and programming languages. It is also worth my while to spend the money to purchase a license (or licenses) for a Content Management System that helps me build a top notch, professional website for my client. Likewise, the professional carpenter will want to keep his toolbox up-to-date with every time-saving and quality-producing tool available on the market; a thousand-dollar electric drill may well be worth the price if it saves ten minutes on each of a thousand tasks.

Which CMS should I use?

It depends on your needs, but one of the most popular CMSs on the market is WordPress. It is free, flexible and pretty easy to learn. In addition, WordPress offers thousands of free website designs (called "Templates" or "Themes") to choose from, as well as countless other fancier designs you can buy from website design companies. If you are not fussy about appearance and want your website up and running quickly for almost no money, WordPress might satisfy you. Even though it is easy to learn, there are lots of technical folks around with WordPress experience who can help you get what you want if you don't want to do the development work yourself.

Drupal and Joomla are two other comparable CMSs. They are less ubiquitous, but offer more technical power under the covers, if you need it, and they are also free.

WordPress, a one-size-fits-all product, is the most commonly used CMS, and it is free[19]. If you're planning to create a single website on a limited budget, WordPress may be enough. Websites created using WordPress tend to look a bit similar, though – in some cases you can recognize a WordPress website instantly – but this might be fine if it is your first foray onto the Internet for a business that is in its early stages; you can keep your costs to a minimum while you prove that you have a business, then revisit the website issue a few years later.

ExpressionEngine and Big Medium are less common, have fewer off-the-shelf templates, but offer significant control over everything a website could be asked to do. ExpressionEngine costs a bit more than Big Medium, but has more features, including a wider variety of design templates to pick from and a built-in community feature.

_____

19 Nothing is ever free, of course, but in computer software shareware of open-source terms, you can use such "free" software as long as you don't violate a number of the software provider's restrictions. You'll have little problem staying within those restrictions, but it's worth it to read up on them for any CMS software you intend to use.

Three reasons to chose ExpressionEngine over Big Medium are (1) ExpressionEngine has a built-in website community feature, (2) it is likely you will find a design template for ExpressionEngine to get you started, saving you days or weeks of work and (3) there is now a significant independent EE development community that can help you if you are stuck.

If you want to built a website that behaves like it cost $100,000, then one of these two CMSs might be the one to choose. Because there are so many CMS systems on the market, and new players coming onto the market all the time, you should be able to find one that fits your needs.

Are "free" CMSs worth what you pay for them?

Because WordPress, Joomla and Drupal are free to use, there is an implicit problem with support.

If you are embarking on a million-dollar business venture, are you prepared to use a "free" Content Management System to build it? WordPress is free; Big Medium is about $200, and ExpressionEngine can cost $500 for the top version. I wouldn't know who to call if I had a problem with the actual WordPress product, but I can easily find vendor support for either Big Medium or ExpressionEngine. That is because the companies that developed them have paid employees to answer the phone and solve problems. Still, I use WordPress occasionally, but I would look for a sharper knife if I am building a serious business website.

That might sound like a minor risk, but consider this eventuality: You pay an independent developer to build your business website, and he goes out of business some time later. You need support for your website, and the developer cannot be found so you get help from another developer. If needed, he or she can contact the vendor of the CMS for support in order to solve your problem and move forward, IF your CMS is a paid-for product. If your website was developed using a free CMS (like WordPress, Joomla or Drupal), you may not be able to find someone who will take responsibility for the functioning of the software – that is – the CMS program itself.
It is a risk worth noting.

What does your website need to do?

Some websites will be static. That is, once you build them, they stay the same for years before being replaced by another one or going away altogether. Others require a great deal of flexibility from the beginning as they grow and change to meet evolving business needs.

The client websites I build are in the $10k - 100k range, and I use either Big Medium or ExpressionEngine almost exclusively for every one of them. Still, I don't want to get religious about it, because every website development project has different requirements, and if you select the CMS that is best suited to the job, it can make a huge difference to the effort you put into the project. If you contact me on www.sboseries.com and tell me what kind of website you are trying to build, I may be able to suggest one for you, or at least, give you some ideas to consider during your decision process.

Sometimes, the organization you pay to build your website has a specific CMS it uses, and may not offer you an alternative. That might be perfectly reasonable, especially if it specializes in a particular type of client and if your requirements are similar to other clients' requirements. If you are reading this book, however, it is probably because you don't know yet what you need, or even what questions to ask. So let me describe the typical platform tiers that web solutions fit into:

Tier 1: Basic blog website

If you have no money to spend and little technical skill, you can create you own blog for free, using one of a number of online blogging packages. For the moment, let's talk about how one of the more common of these works. It's called Blogger and is provided for free by Google.

If you visit www.blogger.com you can follow some simple steps to create your own blog using a name of your choice. You also get to decide what your subdomain name is. What is a subdomain? (More on the significance of subdomain on page 172) Oversimplifying a little, it is the text that goes in front of the main domain name (blogspot.com).
For example: product-trajectory.blogspot.com is a subdomain of blogspot.com.

Whoever owns the domain name owns the content. Google owns the domain name blogspot.com so, in theory at least, they could lay claim to the content of your blog if its address is on a subdomain of blogspot.com. This might not be a problem, but again, in theory, Google could decide in the future to scrap the domain name. If that happens, your subdomain name would disappear with it. It's unlikely of course that Google would destroy the blogspot.com domain, but it is important to understand the implications of a for-profit organization having that kind of control over your content. They could decide to use all of the blogs (each living in its own respective subdomain) under their blogspot.com domain as advertising engines, for which Google takes most or all of the profit. I'm not saying they're likely to do that, but they could if they wanted to. In contrast, owning your own domain (e.g. siteleads.net) is a direct agreement with the government. It could be said that the US Government owns the top-level domain .com or .net, and so on. They won't interfere with your ownership of your domain as long as you renew it every year.

A basic blog like that offered on blogspot.com is a quick and easy way to get your content up onto the Internet without spending any money. It does offer some customization options but if you plan to do anything fancy beyond the basic look-and-feel options in blogspot.com, consider going for the next tier, below.

You still can have your own domain name (for example, *myfancystore.com*) that "points" to your blog myfancystore.blogspot.com. If you do use a primary domain name to reference the underlying blog, it might make it easier to move the blog later, and still preserve all the links from all over the Internet, as long as you promote your blog using that primary domain name (myfancystore.com) and not the subdomain (myfancystore.blogspot.com).

Tier 2: The WordPress "Commons"[20]

If you want your website to look and behave more like a website – and are not satisfied with just a basic blog and the restrictions that implies – the WordPress organization offers a fairly complete website with all the look-and-feel, navigation and content options you'd expect in a website. Your website would live in a subdomain, e.g. *myfancystore*.wordpress.com, eliminating the need to purchase and maintain your own domain.

With the WordPress Commons model, you would not have ultimate control over your domain, because the domain (wordpress.com) is owned by a non-governmental organization. Most of what they offer is free, but they do charge for custom features and design changes if you ask them to do the work for you.

The WordPress Commons model offers a lot more flexibility and configuration options than blogspot.com. It is also evolving and improving at a much faster rate – it seems for the moment at least – than blogspot.com. All of the features on the core product WordPress (see next tier, below) are available to you.

You can use a primary domain name (e.g. myfancystore.com) to "point" to your wordpress.com website (e.g. myfancystore.wordpress.com).

---

20 The WordPress "Commons" is a term I coined to describe the hosting service offered by wordpress.com. It is so called because all the blogs and websites within it share the same primary domain name, wordpress.com

Tier 3: WordPress Website, hosted by a hosting company

There is also an *open source*[21] program called WordPress. It's been around for years and most established website hosting companies[22] offer WordPress as a standard on their servers. It's also usually already installed, so you don't even have to worry about that.

WordPress is the most commonly used Content Management System in the world. It is flexible, easy to learn and has a big developer following.

The down side of WordPress is that websites created with it tend to look rather similar to one another. In fact, as I mentioned earlier, it is usually obvious when you look at a website that it was created using WordPress, unless you have done considerable redesign work to make it look different.

Because WordPress is a one-size-fits-all type of program, it does many thing well, but few things excellently.

WordPress, it could be said, is the ideal program to use if you are creating a website for a mom-and-pop store, have a

---

21 Open source software is written by volunteers and made available to the general community. It's not "free" as such, but for most purposes, you can use it without any charge whatsoever. There are agreed-upon restrictions on the use and dissemination of it, but they are not onerous unless you plan to resell the software itself. Check the legal small print when you install it.

22 A website hosting company is a for-profit organization that stores your website on a server, publishes it to the World Wide Web, and provides you – the website owner – with all the tools and programs you need to manage your website. For example, email management, basic website traffic reports, spam filters and so on.

budget in the hundreds of dollars, and have a little technical skill.

Tier 4: Joomla, Drupal, etc., website, hosted by a hosting company

Joomla and Drupal are like WordPress, but offer more flexibility and power for those who are more technical. With these, you can control more of the look-and-feel of your website. That power comes at a price; you need a little more technical knowhow to take advantage of the extra features.

Joomla and Drupal are both *open source* (described in footnotes), and are often pre-installed by hosting companies.

They don't have as large a technical support base as WordPress has, but do have a wide range of off-the-shelf plug-ins you can drop into your website for extra functionality, for example, shopping baskets, membership forums and so on.

Generally speaking, consider one of these programs if you are going to be spending most of your time working on websites, as it takes a significant time investment to understand how to use either of them.

Tier 5: Specialized CMS program for specific requirements

The next level of Content Management System is one designed for technically sophisticated websites or those that require a website that is very friendly to search engines.

Two examples are Big Medium and ExpressionEngine. Neither is free, but the price is chump change compared to the power they deliver to the develop that needs it.

As I covered earlier in this book, a Content Management System actually makes the website pages for you, compared to a HTML Editor which allows you to build and adjust every page individually. One of the Big Medium product's greatest features is that it creates web pages that are 100% search engine friendly. That means that search engines (e.g. Google, Bing, Yahoo, MSN Search, and many others) can read all of the content within all of the website's pages easily. ExpressionEngine is similar. With other CMSs, that is not always the case. Often, web page content is obscured by embedded scripts and styles, making it more challenging for search engines to find the content within a given page.

A typical comparison of a page created by Big Medium and one created by WordPress results in a page that is about half the size. That means less work for search engines; everything they see is relevant to possible future search matches, resulting in the web page appearing higher up in search results.

In my own website development business, I use Big Medium and ExpressionEngine almost exclusively because the top priority of each of my clients is to appear high up in search results. Competition for top position has gotten so tough over the past few years, it is an advantage I have to have.

In addition to creating immaculate web pages, ExpressionEngine and Big Medium have a number of features that reduce the time required to put the correct keywords in the optimal place for search engines. So, the time you spend adding content gives you a better return on your investment – in terms of search engine visibility – than any other CMS I know of.

It does take a bit of time to get up to speed on the power tools of these CMSs. Working with an organization or an individual who can help you get the most out of your CMS will be advantageous.

What to look for in a Content Management System

Let's look again at what a CMS needs to do for you:

- Separate you from direct access to your website, forcing you to adhere to standards of content creation and maintenance in order to preserve the quality, reliability and consistency of your website's content, structure and appearance.

- Multiple people can add, change or delete content at the same time without colliding with one another.

- Each contributor can be given a different level of access to the website. For example, a "Publisher" might be able to add, change and delete pages through the website – or indeed, a specified section of it – while Writers of Editors may only be able to prepare content for publication.

- Links back and forth through the website are maintained automatically as pages are created, moved, changed or deleted.

- Content should be stored separately from Style Sheets[23] and (usually) scripts[24].

What should my website look like?

The CMS you use – or your website supplier uses – will have a significant influence on what you can reasonably do to the appearance of your new website. Still, with any of the five CMSs I listed above, you can at least develop a website that looks exactly how you want it to look.

Art projects and science experiments

Let me begin by relating to you my experience of delivering websites to the thirty or so most recent clients of mine, covering about the last three years.

For those clients who knew exactly what they wanted their new website to look like, I completed the project on the first attempt. For those who were vague about what they wanted, it often took my company three or four complete attempts – the earlier of which were scrapped – before starting the design all over again. So you'll understand when I tell you, I don't begin any development work now until my client and I have agreed on *exactly what the website will look like*. When I don't enforce that at the beginning, the project inevitably becomes an *art project*,

---

23 Style Sheets, or "Cascading Style Sheet" (CSS) are files that control the general look and feel within a website. For example, how a header is to appear (font name, size, color, etc.).

24 Scripts are like small programs that run inside a given web page. For example, you might want an order total field to change when a product order quantity changes. That piece of script is kick-started any time the order quantity field is changed.

the biggest time wasting phenomenon in the known universe.

Instead, we determine up front *which existing website on the Internet we are going to copy.*

This up front choice (which website we will copy) has several benefits:

1. Everyone on the project – my team and my client's team – knows exactly what the new website is going to look like, and no one is surprised or disappointed when it arrives.

2. The time-to-completion is predictable.

3. We only have to do it once.

So, how do you decide what it should look like? How do you pick the colors, the menu bars and page footers? If you are to design a website from scratch, there sure are a lot of questions to answer!

Did you ever go to a hairdresser with a vague idea of how you'd like her to cut your hair? Every time I went to a hairdresser with a vague idea of what kind of haircut I wanted, I ended up with a vague haircut. A much better idea is to open up a copy of *The Hair Gazette* and show the hairdresser a picture of exactly what I want, by pointing at a picture of a man with the haircut I want. That makes it easy for everyone. And no matter what haircut I could think of, someone in *The Hair Gazette* has thought of it already.

It's the same for website development. My client and I sit down in our office for a few hours and comb through (no pun intended) dozens of real, live websites on the Internet and pick one to use as our *base design*. Then we cherry pick individual elements from other websites and add them as addenda to the base design. For example, we might make the menu bar font larger, the footer background a lighter shade of blue, and so on. I go into this is detail on page 80.

This whole process begins before I ever agree to the development project in the first place. I ask the client to scour the Internet before the meeting – or we do it as a team – and gather a list of their favorite websites. I don't even give the client a project price quotation until I know what we're copying.

We might have a second sit-down meeting if we don't pick one out during the first meeting, but the process is straightforward and it is productive. I've never had a client disappointed with the end result when we started the process like this.

I have an engineering background. I love to tinker with software tools until the wee hours of the morning and I love an art project that allows me to experiment with the latest technologies to see if I can come up with something really cool. Still – and possibly because of that – I have to be careful about getting pulled into what could only be described as an *Art Project from Hell*. In the context of website development, an *Art Project From Hell* is one where you keep trying different ways of doing something until all your time and money are used up, long before the project has produced a working result.

There once was a man who caught a leprechaun and forced him to divulge where his pot o' gold was buried – *under a lone dandelion weed growing in the middle of this field*, the leprechaun is coerced to divulge – and also to swear he would not disturb the dandelion until his captor returned with a shovel. With that sworn promise secured, the man released the leprechaun and ran to his tool shed to fetch a shovel. When he returned, there were *thousands* of dandelions, and every time the man dug one up, another two dandelions would spring out of the ground in its place! Soon the field was covered in dandelions, and the man was forced to give it up altogether and go home empty-handed, cursing the leprechaun every step of the way.

A website development project that does not have a precise design agreement at the beginning is like that field of dandelions. Digging just makes everything worse.

If you want your website development project to be successful, agree on the visual design before your team or web developers start any development work. The more specific the visual design, the less pain everyone will experience.

This process works not simply because you get the design process out of the way early. It works because it forces you and your team to agree on what you want, in other words, what you want your company to look like in public.

Some companies don't know what they want to look like. Rest assured, in those cases, anyone you ask to build your website won't know either.

This principle was true of computer programming thirty years ago and it is true of website design today. Whether you wish to create the website yourself or pay someone to do it for you, shake hands on a digital copy – an existing website, an image file, a PowerPoint slide, or a few screen shots - of the website design you want before you begin work. That way, you won't be left standing alone with a bad haircut in a field, cursing leprechauns.

Let's look at an example of how much more expensive it can get if you begin the project without nailing down the details first. We'll take just one of the web pages you need on your new website; the *User Registration* page:

You ask your web development company (let's call them the "Vendor") to include a User Registration page on your new website. You're not quite sure what fields will be required, but you give them instructions to go ahead and set one up anyway. To make the new page work, the vendor takes a *best guess* at it based on work they did for a different client a year earlier. They add the necessary fields, make a few additions to the database, and program the new page to behave the way they think it should. They spend a couple of days refining the new page, making sure everything lines up, the logo is in the right place, the length of the page doesn't disturb the template, etc., and generally fixing up dozens of look-and-feel issues to make the page fit with the overall website.

A few weeks go by and you (the website owner) do a few tests on the new User Registration page only to realize it's missing a few fields. That is, several questions you need answers to are missing. You communicate the required changes to the vendor and they dutifully open up the project again and add the new fields.

There are several significant problems with this turn of events:

1. Most of the fit-and-finish work they originally did on the User Registration page can be thrown away. The few days your vendor spent on that fit-and-finish cost you $1,500 then, and now it has to be done a second time.

2. Your vendor will spend at least *some* time rediscovering where they were in the project two weeks earlier. The more often a development issue is revisited like this, the messier everything becomes, as developers tend to be more diligent the first time round and more frustrated on subsequent visits to the same project.

The previous example outlines the case of just one simple page of your website. As the overall complexity of the website grows, the cost of not being specific increases exponentially.

Because elements of a complex website take more time than those of a simpler website, that same User Registration page will have consumed four days of development instead of just two. In addition, more pages and more design issues will be involved, so wasted effort increases in all directions. And at some point, the project may have to be abandoned. At the very least, the project incurs cost overruns and is delivered late.

Save yourself a lot of grief. Copy another company's website.

But isn't copying someone else's website illegal? I hear you ask.

Let me tell you, no matter what design you could come up with on your own, someone somewhere has already designed it. With a billion websites on the Internet – well, at least, tens of millions – if you come up with a half-decent website, it has already been done somewhere else. In any case, by the time you *go into production*[25], your new website will have lost enough similarity to the original website you copied. Also, when you are looking for a website to copy, select one used by an organization that does not compete in any way with you.

If you are still worried about making the copy look too much like the original, talk to your attorney about the specific example.

Mercedes versus Hyundai

The cost of designing any given model of the Mercedes-Benz E-Class is probably in the hundreds of millions of dollars; certainly in the tens of millions. Aside from the direct engineering design and related pre-production costs, a thorough marketing analysis project is executed to determine the optimal product quality-feature-cost mix of everything that should go into a car of that caliber. Mercedes-Benz's origins date back to about 1886. They have survived world wars, recessions, depressions, bisection and unification, and have consistently delivered some of the most desired automobiles in the world. It's safe to say, they know what they are doing when it comes to designing a car that will sell.

Half way round the world, a smaller, younger company, Hyundai – in a country a fraction of the size of Germany -

---

25 "In production" is when a product or system is in live use.

decides to enter the luxury car market. What they come up with is a car – the *Genesis* – that looks remarkably like the Mercedes-Benz E-Class. It's so similar, I often get them mixed up whenever I see one in the distance. I have test-driven both and I would say the Hyundai might actually be better than the Mercedes in many respects. Of course, it doesn't have the good-as-gold Mercedes *brand*, but you can't argue with the brilliance of knocking off an original.

Imitation is the sincerest form of flattery

The chaps at Hyundai have been in the business long enough to know that, coming up with their own original look-and-feel – especially for their first entry into the luxury car market in which they wanted to compete for the first time – would be prohibitively expensive. Toyota, through their luxury Lexus brand, have the muscle to do it, but Hyundai doesn't. At least, not yet. And so, Hyundai did what every wise smaller player does: copy the leader in the space.

Skin in the game

Another advantage to a company being *forced to decide what their own website will look like* is, they get involved in the project early. Before you – if you are their supplier – get involved, in fact. And so, the website's owner's contribution to the success of the project begins early.

Many of my clients have told me how challenging it was for them to select a website for us to copy. Even when they narrowed it down to a half dozen candidates, they found it difficult to make the final decision. Whatever chance they have of coming up with one they like, just think how unlikely it would be for you to be successful doing it for them! The moment your client – or whoever will own the new website – chooses the one to copy, they have have made an investment in the success of the project; in modern parlance, they have *skin in the game*. That is, they have their investment in time and energy to lose, and they share the responsibility for the success of the project from the outset.

That's good for everyone.

The one-day rule

After thirty years in software development, I've noticed a pattern in project risk in projects with a large visual component. (Actually, I first noticed the pattern around the year 1999. For a third of those years, I worked on reporting solution development, that is, software products that provide specific visual insights into activities of one type or another in an organization. By way of example, one of my bigger projects was in Bocada Inc, where the software I designed gave information on the success and failure rates of data backups.)

The pattern I noticed was that, *if you can't develop a prototype within one day, the chances of project success decrease precipitously*. "One Day" is a typical day at the office.

By prototype, I mean a convincing visual mock-up of what the application could look like when the product ships. Yes, the product's appearance may change significantly between that first day and shipping day, but that initial, credible prototype proves that there is *at least one plausible path to success from where you are today*.

For software products, to ship a "Version 1.0" in eighteen months, the milestones might look like this: Prototype in one day, refined prototype in one week, working prototype in one month, fully functional product in nine months, tested and reliable product in fifteen months, and beta testing for another three months brings you to a ship date eighteen months after the initial prototype. You see, nothing really starts until that first prototype is agreed upon. It is the rough map to your destination point, so it makes sense that starting without it will result in wasted effort.

And so, there is a strong correlation between the *time it takes to develop the first prototype* and the *time it takes to complete the entire project*. If the prototype takes one day, you get your finished product in X months. If you take a week to develop the first prototype, the product ship date might be five times longer – too far into the future for the project to be worth it. More importantly, *confusion of purpose* is what makes that initial step five times the size it should be, and that confusion of purpose (i.e., no one knows where the destination is) is the seed of destruction, sown in the first week of the project. Moral of the story: *develop a prototype of your website within a single day*, even if it is images you have dummied up in Photoshop or PowerPoint.

In website development, this One Day Rule may be even more applicable than in software projects in general. Certainly, when you start with an existing website as a baseline of where you want to go, you know two things for sure: (1) someone, somewhere was able to put it together and (2) they found it worthwhile to stick with it until completion. Those facts alone significantly increase your chances of project success.

How do you apply the one day rule to your website development project?

If you personally are doing the actual website development work, set aside a single workday when you know you won't be interrupted, and get all the major parts of your website look-and-feel working. It doesn't have to be fully functional – just make sure it generally *looks the way you want it to look*. If you are making the website based on computer images supplied by someone else – a colleague or a client – use those images as a step-by-step guide to select colors and high-level design.

The One-Day Rule applies to from-the-ground-up designs. Many of you will opt for a low cost, off-the-shelf solution – for example, using a website template provided by a website hosting company or software package – in which case, the risk to project completion is almost zero, at least, in terms of design and navigation structure. In those cases, you may well have an entire, completed website within a few hours (without the content of course).

For organizations with more complex requirements – such as a need to build a specific brand – off-the-shelf templates are unlikely to be enough.

Chapter 5 - Going live with your new website

Going live is only the beginning

When I build a website for a client, I'm usually fairly intensely involved for about four to six months. After that, it does taper off a little, but that "tapering off" does not happen at the point of exposing the new website to the public. *Au contraire.* Making the website public marks the *beginning* of the project – a point in time when many of the significant refinements begin to get done.

There is a conversation I have early in the engagement with almost every new client. It goes like this: I remind my client's team (which might be only one person) that "it is time to begin adding content to the new website" as scheduled. Their response is, *but it's not ready!!!! What if someone sees it in this condition? What if our competitors find out what we are doing? Hey, Liam, I think we are far from ready to go live and in fact, I'd like to take the whole thing offline until we are ready. What's more, I am disappointed in how unfinished the whole website is.*

Even though, before we even sign contracts, I describe at every opportunity the "Go Live" process to my client, people just get nervous about exposing their "unfinished" website to the world. The fact is, your website will always be unfinished. That is to say, a successful web presence includes a website that is always in need of change, and that is a good thing. It is not like a car which, when it rolls off the production line, had better be finished. Neither is it like a software program that gets released as *version number such-and-such*. It is like a tree being planted. You want an oak tree in your yard? The sooner you plant your sapling, the sooner you get the oak tree. And, to stretch the metaphor further, an oak tree will continue to grow and grow for every day of its life.

Being seen in public

My client – or any client – will reasonably feel that the website is not ready at "Go Live". A kind of panic sets in at the point where they must begin adding significant content to their website or truly interacting through their website with the world outside.

One client – this very day, in fact – explained to me that, the day I set her about adding products to her new website, she felt like she was "abandoned in her underwear, in the center of town". (Mind you, I did dwell on that for a few fleeting moments. But I digress). A few weeks later, she appreciated fully what the value of *Going Live Early* was: the pressure was on to make improvements, and that rate of improvement accelerated significantly once the website went public.

A website that sits securely on some server, hidden from the world, is useless. It's like having an acorn (the seed for an oak tree), sitting in a bag in your garage.

When the first content arrives in a new website, a kind of germination takes place, and the website status goes from being *Static* to being *Dynamic*. The equivalent inflection point in biology is called *quickening*[26].

Having a web presence is like having a family, and the quickest way to start a family is to get pregnant. Sure, we all want ideal circumstances before we bring a child into the world; the house with the picket fence, the savings in the bank, the car paid off, and so on. But all those mechanical preparations don't start a family. They might make life easier, but any parent will tell you, getting pregnant is when the clock starts ticking. That same parent may also tell you it is easy to leave it so late, you may lose the opportunity entirely, or you may compromise your chances of success entirely.

And so it is with your web presence. Get pregnant early.

When you have started your new family by getting pregnant, you can circle back and remodel that den into a nursery, or go shopping for a car seat or stock up on diapers or go on a parenting course. But just like starting a family, your website presence won't be born until some time *after* the first website content is exposed to the world. It is only after that event that search engines begin to see what you have and the real action begins. Even then, it takes time. Search engines take their sweet time to comb through what you have published and sometime after that, you may begin to appear in search results. And probably long after that – if indeed it ever happens – you might appear on the first page of search results. So get started early.

---

26 Dictionary says: Quickening: to begin to manifest signs of life, as in *The spring rains quickened the earth*.

Even without having a clue about what being a parent was, I didn't feel ready when I knew my wife was expecting our first child. I expect, most people don't feel ready to have children once they know the event is imminent. Heck, I've got two teenage kids and an eleven year-old and I still don't feel ready to be a parent, but that is Nature's way of always pushing the program to the limit; you're not ready, but you go ahead anyway.

One of my clients called me to say that her friend in California called her to say there were grammatical errors in the text of her bio page on her new website. Initially shocked by the danger of it all, that same friend offered to write her bio for her. It was a great example of how a website improves when the world gets to see it.

And so, your website has got to experience that *day of the quickening*. You *should* feel a bit anxious. If you don't, perhaps you haven't yet grasped the enormity of what you have taken on. In addition, if there is no market for what you provide, the sooner you find that out, the better. So even in the case where there is no possibility of success, it is better to find that out sooner rather than later; get whatever you have to offer up on your website and let the show begin.

How to calculate the ROI of your website

If you spend $25k on a shiny new website, and lots of profitable sales were to quickly flow into your business through it, you could easily calculate your Return on Investment (ROI). But I have never seen a situation where profitability was so easy to calculate.

A profitable website – I should really say *web presence* – is deeply woven into the business that owns it. For example: a phone call to the business may result in an online purchase, an online search on your website may result in a phoned-in order, or a long worked-on deal with a customer may have been secured after the customer researched your business through your website. The fact is, your website can help your business in many, many ways. One of my clients sells high-end European furniture. His website serves as a kind of brochure to prospective clients, where they can browse images, descriptions and prices before deciding to buy. The website is a significant aid to closing person-to-person deals, even though such deals do not show up in the website's electronic shopping cart.

So, how do you calculate your ROI? I like to ask the question in reverse. *How much business will you lose if you don't have a web presence that reflects the quality product or service you are trying to sell?*

It is hard to imagine a business today that does not need a web presence. They are not just for high tech companies or retail giants. Last week in my local public library, for the first time, I met a homeless man who had his own website. He was living out of a station-wagon, hadn't taken a shower in months, but had a small website throwing off a few hundred dollars in affiliate sales commissions every month. When homeless people feel the need to have an online presence, you have to ask yourself, what risk are you taking by not having one?

The short answer to the question of this chapter is, it is difficult to calculate the return on investment for a website. With some types of small businesses, you can easily see how it contributes to the success of the business. I have several clients who, for years, have been relying exclusively on the lead generation from their simple website. Larger than one-person organizations usually have a more difficult time working out the exact payback because an individual's effort can contribute to – or benefit from – the success of the business's web presence without anyone knowing it. Still we can list the ways in which a website can support your business. Some are concrete; some are subtle:

- Direct revenue from the website through the sale of products.

- Sales in your bricks-and-mortar business from people who found you through your web presence (website, Facebook, Twitter, etc.).

- Word-of-mouth referrals by people passing links to your website, products, articles, Facebook, etc..

- Business validation by prospects examining the quality and depth of your online content.

I'm no arborist, but I would safely bet that an oak tree gains more weight in its fifth year of growth than it does in its first year of growth. Each year, up to a point, the amount of weight a tree gains increases. Consider the paltry few ounces an oak tree might gain in its first year, as it grows from an acorn into a sapling, and compare that to just the weight of all the leaves you sweep up in the Autumn from a mature oak tree. It might shed five leaves in its second year of growth, hundreds of leaves in its fifth year, and tens of thousands of leaves in its twentieth year.

The math of web presence growth works like that of the oak tree. Yes, you will see progress in the first year, but the real payoff is in the long term, so keep your eye on, and invest in, the long term benefits of having an established and profitable web presence.

The long tail

According to Wikipedia, *The ... long tail refers to the statistical property that a larger share of population rests within the tail of a probability distribution than observed under a 'normal' or Gaussian distribution.*

In plain English, it means your return on investment begins to manifest later, but continues to payoff well into the future, compared to an investment in an equivalent bricks-and-mortar business. The *long tail effect* applies to the return you can expect across the lifetime of a web presence, unlike the return you can expect when you open a physical bricks-and-mortar store.

> *The return on investment in an organization's web presence is subject to the long tail effect*

Unfortunately, the long tail effect is counter-intuitive to most of us. We invest $30,000 in our new website, add a bunch of products and expect the sales to flow. Why wouldn't they? After all, they began selling the exact same products in our physical store the day the doors opened.

There certainly are ways to speed things up. Just like the Oak tree which can be nurtured with fertilizers and growth-promoting chemicals, giving it a major boost at the beginning of its life, a website can be promoted to get more targeted traffic by spending money on ads, Search Engine Optimization services, a world class Content Management System, premium content and of course online advertising. But you can't grow a mature Oak tree in one year any more than you can create a mature online web presence (a brand, actually) in a year.

Is your market local or further away?

A "local" market is one that is within driving distance. Is your business close enough for customers to drive to your business to avail of your product or service? If the answer is Yes, then the time it takes to start seeing your return on investment will be shorter than if your target market is non-local.

> On the Web, the return on investment in a local
> market begins sooner than in a non-local market

How can that be? *Why does it take longer to see the first profits in a market that is further away,* I hear you ask. *I thought that was what the Internet was all about,* you exclaim.

Building a brand means building trust. Have you ever noticed how different a business relationship can be after you meet the person for the first time? I have been acquainted with people for years from a distance, only to meet them one day in person for the first time and suddenly, the relationship takes on a whole new meaning. Real trust begins to grow when you look someone in the eye and they into yours. When your customers have in-person experience of you – for instance, by visiting you in your physical store – your brand (which, remember, lives in their mind) becomes much stronger.

In terms of *how long it takes,* it is an order of magnitude more difficult to create a valuable brand when your target market has never met you. This is why it takes so much time to get that return on investment on your website when your target market is not within driving distance.

> *It takes a long time for your return on investment to begin when your target market is not within driving distance*

The bad news is also the good news

Then one day, that first obvious sign of a return-on-investment arrives. It might be a web order, a telephone call or an email, but it is a clear sign that the investment has begun to produce something. It is that "first snowflake of a snow storm". The absolutely wonderful thing about the *long tail effect* is that it can pay you back over and over and over. Usually, a little care and attention is all that is needed to keep your web presence profitable once the returns have begun to appear.

A friend of mine in a city in Illinois owns a traditional bricks-and-mortar jewelry store. The store itself is doing quite well. A competing business across town has a clearly inferior physical store, but the owners have been applying themselves to the business of creating a web presence to sell their products nationally for a number of years. Over the course of the last five years, that competitor quietly added products for sale to their website every day. As each product got sold – through the website or from the physical store – they would simply put a *sold* sign on that product in the website, but leave all of its content (pictures, description, pricing, specification, etc.) on the website for all to see. Each sold product would therefore continue to attract search traffic. Even if a person looking for a "lady's 1995 diamond studded Rolex watch" lands on that sold product page on this website, they may end up buying something else. In addition, the sheer bulk of relevant content around the subject of pre-owned jewelry raises the value of the entire website in the eyes of search engines. Today, the website has some ten thousand products visible on the site, although only a few dozen are actually for sale at any time. That business has created an effective and profitable web presence by sticking to the process of adding at least some content every day. It is the gift that keeps on giving and more so as it continues to grow. Adding a mere five new items for sale every day, has brought them close to ten thousand products on their website today. In making that investment, the following has taken effect:

1. A massive array of Secondary Target Landing Pages is present on their website.

2. The sheer number of products visible on their website sends a strong signal to visitors that they are dealing with an established business.

3. Search engines will favor their pages over pages from websites with fewer pages.

4. Selling products on their own website means they retain the commissions usually payable on websites such as eBay and others.

5. Such an impressive website drives local customers to their physical store because they almost always appear at the top of search results for related searches locally.

If you have true faith in the value of the product or service you bring to your target market, you will also have faith that it will stand the test of time. When your web presence begins to bear fruit, know that it is just the beginning of a long and profitable journey as foretold by the *long tail effect*.

Bricks to Clicks

Chapter 6 - Advertising

"Buying one dollar with five"

Riddle: *"You can't eat it, it doesn't improve a product, it doesn't make customers happier, but billions are spent on it. What is it?"*

Why, it's *Advertising*, silly!

The problem I have with advertising is that it doesn't create any real value. Great, if it introduces your product to a prospect and it results in a sale, but an advertisement itself does not make a product or service better, or transport you across town. You can't eat it, and once you buy it, your money is gone forever.

One of the reasons old fashioned print advertising revenue dropped off so precipitously when the Internet showed up was, the Internet showed marketers how effective (or ineffective) an ad campaign was; it can often tell you exactly how much revenue resulted from a specific advertisement. Still, not all advertising is meant to drive immediate sales. It is often an investment in *brand awareness* or *product category ownership.* For example: I might be in the market for a new car twelve months from now. As I read online newspapers, browse through my email and generally surf the 'net today, I see ads everywhere. I can't say I remember many of them – and effective ads are perhaps the ones you forget – but they do have an effect on the choice of car I will make next year. So, the best return on investment on paid advertising is probably for the *long term reinforcement of brand value in the buyer's mind.*

Such long term investment in advertising must be hard to measure, especially for established companies, who have countless marketing campaigns running at the same time. Who is to say which ad worked and which did not? Likely, as long as the company's overall success continues, advertising expenditure is allowed to continue, and it's not until there is a shortage of money that corporate officers try to determine how effective their advertising is. And perhaps large corporations can work it all out – sort the pepper from the sparrow droppings, as it were – but my observations tell me, it is difficult, if not impossible, to make paid advertising profitable for the small business selling to a global market over the Internet.

When there is no reliable way to measure a specific ad's effectiveness, a lot of money can be spent on it in the sheer hope that something comes of it. Perhaps it is a mix of corporate habit and enthusiastic advertising sales reps that keeps the time-honored tradition of advertising alive. To me, advertisers are more often like roosters: They tell you their crowing makes the sun rise.

Any advertising campaigns I've ever looked at produced a poor return; usually in the order of, for every five dollars spent, one dollar is made. Still, some companies do make their advertising pay off. You just need to watch it and measure it.

There are many ways to advertise on the Internet: Google AdWords (or equivalent), bulk email campaigns and affiliate marketing, to name but three. If you decide to put money into advertising, get together with an advertising expert you trust.

How do *Google AdWords* work?

The vast bulk of Google's profit continues to come from online advertising. They recently called themselves an "advertising company" (although I would call them an advertising technology company, which is something quite different. In fact, I don't think they know any more about *advertising* than you or I do, but they sure as hell know how to enable others to get their ads in front of prospects.)

Google AdWords is a way for companies to bid for advertising space. You might sign up, for example, to *pay up to 50c every time someone clicks your ad* when the words *dry cleaning manhattan* are searched for in a given geographic location. Google then tries to match your ad with specific search terms to maximize the chance someone will actually click your ad, because it is only then that Google makes their money on the ad.

There is quite a science behind such Internet ads – far more than I could cover in this book – so you might study how it works with the help of an online advertising expert, before throwing a lot of money at it. You can set a daily advertising dollar budget for a Google AdWords campaign, so a good way to dip your toe into the proverbial river might be to experiment with small amounts of money until you strike a winning formula for advertising your product. Before you cash in your retirement plan.

Bricks to Clicks

Chapter 7 - Your social media strategy

Buying time

My two sons and I, in the middle of winter this last year, climbed over a high fence to get into our apartment complex outdoor swimming pool. It was cold, but the sheer flagrance of rules made it all worth while. We made up a competition to see who could stay in the frigid water the longest, and my older son won it easily; he won because he had the staying power. (At fourteen years of age, he was 180 lbs and six foot tall, so that probably helped too).

As my business partners and I were building Bocada, it occurred to us that winning was in great part a question of simply *surviving long enough* to get acquired or go public. We watched a number of followers and similar companies drop off the radar, perhaps as a result of running out of money, running out of ideas or simply running out of will power. Whatever the reason, it became clear we were facing a kind of "last man standing" challenge that picked off the weakest startup in our space one by one until there was one player left: the Winner. Much as we liked to believe early on that it was critical to watch our competitors' moves, it eventually dawned on us that it might be a mistake to copy anything a competitor did; most of them didn't fully understand the market's needs and many were, in fact, copying us. Instead, a dedicated focus on our very own customers and a willingness to "stay in the cold water" longer than anyone else always returned the best results.

It was a game of staying alive. We knew how to improve our product, and what our target market needed. We just had to manage our cash flow – both personal and business – long enough to outlive our competitors, whoever they were, while we continued to bring product value to our target market.

Your Social Media strategy is a part of your overall Internet strategy. Although it is tempting to think there might be a short cut to getting all those nice Twitter Followers or Facebook friends, the truth is, it takes time. You could be lucky and develop a loyal following of thousands of Twitter Followers in a matter of months, but it usually takes a lot longer, even when you dedicate yourself to it.

> *If you are starting your Internet business from scratch, with a hope of eventually making a living out of it, having a secondary source of income while you build it will greatly increase your chances of success*

Time plays a big role in your Internet strategy. It's like planting an acorn and expecting an oak tree to pop right out of the ground. If you don't have the time and resources to wait, you had better be darn lucky.

Blog + Facebook + Twitter

Everyone tells you, you need a Social Media Strategy or it's "Hey Jimmy! How is your Blog strategy going?"
I know I'm sick of hearing it.

At a high level, a Blog/Facebook/Twitter strategy goes like this: *You create a new page in the blog on your website, publish it, mention it – including a link to it – in your special Facebook section you've created for your business. You mention, and link to, the blog posting also in your Twitter account. You do all that every day for a year.* Somewhere along the way, you begin to see results. Yes, it can be infinitely more complex than that, but the basic principle is the same. It's about gathering Followers (Twitter) and Likers (Facebook) until you have a kind of "Californian Church" - lots of mesmerized people who will eagerly eat up your religion when the time comes, and fill the hat with good coin when you pass it round.

Making Twitter generate sales

I have spent a lot of time staring at Twitter, wondering how on Earth it could ever add something to my business or to one of my clients' businesses. My clients and I have done quite a few experiments over the past few years and I've come up with this general approach that works. I hate the phrase *Individual Results May Vary* because it usually means *don't blame us when it doesn't work*, but this may actually work better for you than how I describe it. Your business might be suited to Twitter; not all businesses are.

What types of businesses are most suited to a Twitter strategy?

If your business caters to a longer term interest, or a hobby related product, Twitter will be more useful than if your product (or service) is a commodity. If you sell, for example, a golf training video, fancy model train equipment or unique hand-made silver necklaces, a Twitter strategy can work very well. If you sell replacement water heaters, car detailing services or Christmas trees, it is less likely to be helpful. That is because Twitter (and Facebook) are driven by relationships, and relationships take time. To buy a Christmas tree, you don't go to Facebook or Twitter and follow Christmas tree growers for months before you choose a tree. But if you are considering a motorbike to dull the pain of your mid-life crisis, you may follow Harley-Davidson's Twitter account for three years while you summon the courage to buy one for yourself.

> *Generating a sale from a Follower on Twitter or Facebook is a long term process*

Twitter step-by-step

The following process is a bit simplistic. There are volumes of books written about how to create and use a Twitter account. If you wish to dive in deeper than I cover here, there is an excellent Amazon.com publication titled the _Definitive Twitter Guide_.

- Set up a Twitter account on twitter.com. If your preferred Twitter name (the name of your company or organization) is not already taken, the name of your business (or your own name, if your name is your brand) is what you should call your Twitter account. For example, if you sell hand-made silver necklaces, use the name your current buyers know you by.

You've created a basic Twitter account, and linked it to your website. I won't go into every feature available in Twitter;

just enough for you to get started. You can explore Twitter later, but for now, these are your next steps:

1. Search Twitter for other accounts you might like to "follow[27]". If you are in the golf products business, you might search for people using the search term "golf" or "golf enthusiast". Pick a dozen to follow by clicking the "follow" button for each. Don't worry about identifying the absolutely ideal Twitter accounts to follow just yet. All you need now is to get the hang of this "following" business.

2. Come back the next day and follow another dozen Twitter accounts. Some of these will "follow you back" which means, they have noticed that you are following them and have decided to reciprocate. Do this for about a week. The objective is to *get others to follow you*. You've probably only got a handful of Followers at this point. That's OK. The next steps are meant to grow that following as well as keep your brand fresh in the eyes of all of your Followers.

3. Back on your website, write a blog posting every day[28]. After you publish each new posting, go to your Twitter account and "Tweet[29]" about it with a link back to your blog posting.

---

27 "Following" another Twitter account simply means, when they type something, you see it appearing on your Twitter list whenever you log in to your account on Twitter.

28 People ask me, *will it be enough to do just two or three blog postings per week*? I answer *No, it is better to do one every day*.

29 Tweet: a verb, meaning to make a posting about something on your Twitter account.

For example: You make hand-made chocolates. Every morning, you write a paragraph or two in a new blog posting on your website. Today, you might write about "gifting chocolates to diabetics", tomorrow, it might be about "storing your chocolates for a long time" and the next day, it might be "what you need to know about nut allergies", and so on. If you have a real business, there are hundreds of topics you can talk about. Carve them up into one- or two-sentence nuggets of wisdom and post each one to your website.

Some Content Management Systems (CMS) allow you to schedule each posting for a specific date and time. The CMS then publishes it on your website at the designated time, without you having to log in to publish it manually. If you have such a feature, you could do your blog postings in batches, but by scheduling each to appear on a successive day, your website will look – to search engines as well as visitors and Twitter Followers – like you are active on your website every day. The appearance of new material on your website every day is highly regarded by search engines, and it allows you to get a lot of the blogging drudgery out of the way during the times you are less busy. Each morning, you look at the latest blog entry and mention it in your Twitter account.

The objective of your Twitter strategy is to gather as many Followers as possible and to keep them interested. This is as challenging as trying to get people to hear you in the middle of a Metallica[30] concert. Still, there are ways.

If you do an Internet search for *Twitter Management Programs*, you'll find a number of tools that will help you winnow out those who are not "following you back" when you follow them in your Twitter account. Let's call these Twitter accounts that you followed but did not follow you back "Twitter Non-Reciprocators", TNRs for short here. Generally speaking, you want to follow only those who reciprocate by also *following you back*. Basic Twitter makes it difficult to identify such non-followers, but programs are available to help you identify them quickly, especially when your Follower count runs into the thousands.

So, your daily Twitter process is (1) *Follow, (2) Remove week-old TNRs, (3) Follow more, (4) Repeat.* And remember, another great source of people to follow are *Followers of your Followers*. Such Twitter accounts are twice as likely (as Twitter accounts in general) to reciprocate by following you back. I would guess this is because they are interested in those you follow, so are likely to be similar to your immediate Followers.

What I really like about this model is, it is not *gaming the system[31]*, which so many of these schemes appear to do. By

---

30 Metallica is a rock band – a "heavy metal" band no less. If you've ever been to one of their concerts, you might remember being partially deaf for a few days afterwards. No offense meant to Metallica fans. At my age, everything my kids listen to sounds like a continuous train crash.

31 "gaming the system" is a term for attempts to drive more traffic to your website by tricking the search engines to give you higher rankings.

following your Followers' Followers, you are connecting with people who are far more likely to be interested in hearing from you and following what you are up to. This is a good example of *Inbound Marketing*[32] at work.

An example of a program that can help you increase your Follower count in a way that won't incur the ire of the folks at Twitter is TwitterAdder. As of writing this, their website was www.twitteradder.com. Their program allows you to follow Twitter accounts based on certain keywords in their profile. Presumably, the company that produces TwitterAdder will still be around when you read this.

If you have the patience and discipline to stick with your Twitter growth strategy, it is possible to gather tens of thousands – if not hundreds of thousands – of Followers, each directly interested in what you are doing. Your biggest challenge will be the person who peers back at you when you look into the mirror. Sticking with the drudgery of all this Social Media activity takes serious will power. Most people – probably more that 90% of us – don't have the long-term staying power to stick with it long enough for it to pay off. When it comes to blogging, the vast majority give up after writing their third blog posting.

Let's look at a practical example:

By hand, you make exquisite silver and gold necklaces and bracelets. Up until now, you've been able to sell the odd piece here and there through word-of-mouth. But now, you want to increase revenue by making and selling more units.

---

32 Inbound Marketing is, loosely speaking, the process of attracting prospects through the act of their looking for you, and not, your getting their attention through spam or in-your-face advertising.

You want to turn this hobby into a business. Doing so means getting a business license, paying taxes, and taking the whole thing to a new level of organization and responsibility. So, you need a way of reaching far greater numbers of people than you did when you made and sold one necklace a week. Old-fashioned word-of-mouth is not going to be able to handle the much bigger volume of sales you will need when you are making three necklaces a day. Enter Twitter.

Every time you make a new necklace and want to sell it, you post an announcement to your blog about it – perhaps with a photograph – and Tweet about it with a link back to that blog posting in your Twitter account. You still try to keep your list of Followers growing and growing as word of your creations spreads through the Social Media equivalent of word-of-mouth.

The program I mentioned above, TwitterAdder, would enable you to follow, and gather Followers from, those who have "jewelry" as a keyword in their Twitter profile. With the investment of a few minutes each morning, you could grow your list of Twitter followers substantially over a few months. It could become a meaningful source of leads for your business. Still, remember that Followers for the sake of Followers are not in themselves a winning strategy: they must be interested in, and be able to buy, what you are selling.

Chapter 8 - For website developers

I never planned to get into the business of developing websites for clients. Although I have developed websites for my own businesses over the years, and outsourced the development of other websites, my business has for years been squarely in the area of Search Engine Optimization[33]. One day, a friend asked me to rebuild their business website over a weekend. So, I dove right in, using the tools I knew, but wasn't yet highly skilled in. Before I was even finished that one website, a friend of the client asked me to do another. And for the past three years, I've been developing websites for clients who have been referred to me.

If you are in the business of developing websites for other companies, what skills and tools might you need to be successful?

- – A means to host the actual websites you build. There are dozens of established hosting companies (e.g. bluehost.com, Godaddy.com, Hostgator.com) that charge a fee for server space and related tools. You can sign up at different levels, depending on how much space and bandwidth you need. Typically, they charge a few hundred dollars per year for an account that allows you to support a large number of websites.

---

33 Search Engine Optimization, or SEO for short, is the activities required to get a particular website to display as early as possible in search results.

- Knowledge of how to use one or more Content Management Systems to build and maintain websites. As I mentioned earlier, prices range from *free* to *very expensive*, depending on which one you buy.

- An understanding of things like "add-on domains", "Nameservers", hosting packages, email account management and a bunch of other little bits and pieces that help you solve problems for your clients as they arise. None of it is rocket science, but there are many small things to learn. Probably, though, if you already are a website solution provider, you'll know a lot of it already.

- Basic skills in an image manipulation tool such as Photoshop, Paintshop Pro or Gimp. The alternative is, you rely on a business partner or other resource to handle graphics and related work for you.

If you get the opportunity to build a relatively simple website to begin with, you can use that experience to try more and more challenging website designs and features as you progress to larger clients. Thankfully, my first paying website clients were small, which limited the number of new skills I needed at the beginning. I learned a little more with each new website – and was able to charge a little more – and delivered more as I served larger and larger clients.

Unless you come into this new business with a solid grounding of technical skills, your prices will probably have to start at a modest level, and for clients with modest aspirations, before you work your way up to more and more challenging – and lucrative – opportunities.

Bricks to Clicks

Chapter 9 - Adding new content every day

This is such a key element of your success, it is worth summarizing.

I spend a significant portion of my time perusing Google Analytics reports of my clients' websites. One pattern I see surfacing over and over is this: *Daily addition of new content to a website increases the traffic to that website significantly*.

Sometimes it is more obvious than others. One of my clients relies exclusively on her website to generate new business. She noticed that, about a week after she returns to adding a new blog posting to her website every day, email inquiries resume and the phone starts to ring more often again. And about a week after she *stops* making daily blog postings to her website, new inquiry emails drop off again and the phone stops ringing.

What is going on?

Search engines see websites that regularly have new material as being more valuable than websites that do not. It's pretty obvious, really, when you think about it. A business whose website publishes new material every day is more likely to be an active business. That would be a reasonable assumption, and it is no surprise that search engines favor such busy websites over ones whose material could be described as stale. And so – all else being equal – those websites that publish new material regularly will appear in the list of search results ahead of those websites with stale material. It might be the difference between appearing on the first page of search results versus appearing on page seven of search results. You might think this is an exaggeration, but I see this pattern with most of my clients' websites.

Critically Important: Websites that publish new material every day appear much earlier in search results than websites with stale material!

How long before the "new material" takes effect?

I remember watching a TV show in the 1970s called *The Magician*. Bill Bixby (who also played the "normal" guy in *The Incredible Hulk* series around the same time) played the part. In one episode of *The Magician*, he demonstrated how to throw individual metal playing cards so they would stick into a wooden object like a tabletop. Obviously impressed, the other actor in the episode asked, "How long did it take to learn that trick?". "Thirty minutes", Bixby replied, "every day for four years".

Getting search engines to finally promote your website as a result of daily new material takes somewhere between six and twelve months. That's an approximation, and whether it alone is enough for your website to appear on the first page of search results is another question. But it is necessary. Remember the story of the two friends running away from a pursuing Grizzly bear: one guy exhorted "we'll never outrun this Grizzly", to which the other replied "Who cares. I only have to outrun you". It's the same with your position in search results: You only have to get ahead of your competition. For some of my clients, their competition is not doing the necessary legwork – in which case it is easier for my client to appear ahead of them in search results – and for other clients, their competition is doing everything right and it's a bloody fight for the top slot. No matter what, though, it is unlikely your website will appear at the top of organic search results if it does not publish *at least one new page every day*.

Simple as that axiom sounds, ninety percent of my clients struggle with being able to add that content every day. The obstacles to adding new content are:

- It takes serious discipline to revisit the website every day and type up new content.
  We all have other, more important work to do. There is always a reason to put off, or a distraction from, adding a new page to your website every day. It might be an important customer call or writer's block, but most people abandon the project after three of four new additions to their website.

- It is hard to come up with lots of pieces of new material.

- Most people still feel that everything they add to their website must be perfect, so they spend too much time creating a simple blog entry, or never finish the job because it's never good enough.

Bricks to Clicks

Chapter 10 - Securing your intellectual property

Owning the foundation of your investment

Imagine, for a moment, you visit a local nursery – that is, a place that sells trees and shrubs – and you buy a hundred-dollar Japanese Maple tree. For that money, you'd get one that is likely small enough to fit in the trunk or on the back seat of your car. You take it home and plant it, not in your yard, but in your *neighbor's* yard, where you will be able to see it easily from your own house. Assuming your neighbor doesn't have a problem with you giving him this nice gift, with a bit of luck, you'll be able to enjoy the view of the tree for years to come.

Who owns the tree after it is planted in your neighbor's yard? Do you think it is reasonable for your neighbor to cut down or transplant the tree later if he so desires? Assuming he leaves (no pun intended) the tree to grow – and for you to enjoy indefinitely – what happens if he sells his house? Who owns the tree then?

This hypothetical scenario illustrates a mistake many businesses make when they make investments in content on the Internet: *they don't actually own the property that holds the content.*

How does this happen, and what does it mean to "own the property"?

Every website lives under what is called a domain. An example of a domain is *nytimes.com*. You probably already know that you license a domain name – essentially from the government, who owns the Internet, by the way – by paying a small fee every year. Most people consider this *licensing* of the domain name as really *owning* the domain name, which, for our purposes here, is correct. Even though you pay a yearly fee to remain in control of your domain name, no one can easily take it from you. You decide what website your domain name points to and as long as you pay the paltry fee when it comes due every year, you remain in control of what people see when they visit your website.

The problem is, sometimes people are unaware that all their efforts into putting content onto the web are actually adding value to a domain name that *someone else owns*. For example, I could have spent the last year diligently posting entries to my blog at liamscanlan.blogspot.com. Even though I set that blog up myself, it is actually owned by whatever organization owns the domain blogspot.com.

At first you might not be so worried about that minor detail, but if the owners of the blogspot.com domain name decide to insert their own revenue-generating ads into every page on your blog – a sub-domain of blogspot.com – there's little you can do about it.

Inserting ads into your blog might be the least of your worries. I have seen many cases recently where people invested great effort into amassing considerable intellectual property in another organization's website only to find the carpet whipped out from under them – the owners, for example, deleted their account – losing their entire investment.

It is essential you own the domain name that contains your web content

There are a few unusual circumstances where it makes good business sense to add content to another organization's website or, more specifically, to a domain name you do not own. If you are a freelance writer, for example, an article of yours getting published on the New Your Times website might be very beneficial to you personally. That is because, the New York Times has such an incredibly valuable brand, even walking past it will do you some good.

Plant on my land, please

There are community websites all over the Web, where the owners encourage visitors and members to make postings, upload photos and carry on all manner of conversations. And when visitors do just that – add content to such a community website – they truly are adding real value. The owners of the website – again, more specifically, the people who *own the domain name under the website* – have a number of choices on how to exploit the intellectual capital in the content that everyone has so gradually built up over years.

I've been told on a number of occasions that this ownership of domain name is a largely semantic issue, one that is not nearly as significant as I claim. Let me relate to you a few examples of where ignorance of it has resulted in disappointment.

1. I myself registered on startupnation.com and made a half dozen well thought-out postings to their forum when one morning, to my surprise, my account was deleted. I got an email from their administrator saying my postings were considered "too self-serving".

2. One of my acquaintances in the world of SEO had his Twitter account deleted after he mistakenly passed the threshold of "allowed number of Follows". He had put a lot of work into it – all of which he lost when his account was deleted - before it happened.

3. Another of my acquaintances in the business community had his biznik.com account deleted because his content was "too salesy" (they told him he was focused too much on selling his own services). Unfortunately for him, he had invested a considerable amount of effort over the previous year adding content, driving visitor traffic and publishing Inbound Links to his work before the content was summarily deleted along with his account.

All of these cases involved a situation where the person creating the content did not own the domain upon which they "planted" that content.

Way back in 2007, an attorney friend of mine asked me to do one final pass on the due diligence on a potential acquisition he and his client were about to close. They were about to buy a company for millions of dollars. We sat in Starbucks as I pored over the technical paperwork while examining the soon-to-be-acquired company's online web application – the core of the acquisition value. I wasn't even the official technical due diligence representation for the acquisition. The subject simply came up as an afterthought while we were having coffee. As I examined the company's product, I noticed that the would-be-acquired company did not own the domain name upon which the IP, brand and value were intimately tied. Yes, they could have decoupled it – transplanted the value – *eventually,* but it was enough to derail the acquisition because the company's value was perceived to be compromised.

Organizations that create an online community – and there are many of them, from Facebook to Twitter – benefit *enormously* from others' contributions to their respective websites. They own the data, they control it, and use it in whatever manner they choose. Your First Amendment Rights[34] don't apply to the opinions you place under someone else's domain on the Internet. They can shut you off as easily as turning off a faucet.

Just imagine thousands or even millions of online members adding content to *your* website every day! It is no surprise some of these websites grow to be worth millions or sometimes billions of dollars.

In reality, the Facebook web application is not that complicated. Yes, they have refined it over the years, but to recreate the actual software itself would take a few good engineers a few months. The power of Facebook is not in its amazingly sophisticated software. It is in its *vast amount of interrelated content.* Sitting upon that simple domain

---

34 The right to free speech, if you are protected by the Constitution of the United States.

name 'facebook.com' lies a multi-billion dollar mountain of content. What is that content? It is the network of friends, family and acquaintances tied to billions of messages, photos, emails and other data. And the owners of the domain name facebook.com own all of it, because they own the domain name facebook.com.

The following paragraph is the introduction to an article written by Jessica Guynn in the *LA Times* on April 17 2011. It is titled: *Facebook looks to cash in on user data.*

"Profiles, status updates and messages all include a mother lode of voluntarily provided information. The social media site is using it to help advertisers find exactly who they want to reach. Privacy watchdogs are aghast."

No surprise there. Such a treasure trove of highly integrated and interrelated data is simply too valuable to go unharvested for long. Privacy watchdogs may swoon in horror, but the data – in terms of what rights a person has to use it commercially – belongs to whoever owns the domain name. In Facebook's case, it is the owners of the domain name facebook.com. It would probably take an edict from the United States Supreme Court to change that fact of ownership.

Corporations have been cashing in on private data long before Facebook or the Internet showed up. Banks have for years been selling the contact information of new customers to third parties. You open up a simple deposit account and, lo and behold, a few weeks later a new wave of junk mail starts to show up in your mailbox. The Internet has simply made the process more intrusive and more far-reaching.

I suggest to my clients that, every time they make a posting to a website for which they do *not own the domain name,* they visualize taking a hundred dollars out of their pocket and giving it to the owner of the website. It is the *content* that drives traffic, which in turn drives more visitors to add more content and so on. The value of a website is in its content, in the same way the way the value of a forest is in its trees.

> *The* value *of a website is in its content, in the same way the way the value of a forest is in its trees*

Once a community website (e.g. Facebook.com, Twitter.com, Landroverforum.com, crochetsociety.com, etc.) reaches the threshold of members adding content of their own free will, the website can begin to grow in value very quickly. It is the age-old concept of the *network effect,* but on steroids. Because of the global reach of the Web, a community website, given the right circumstances, can grow to astronomical proportions.

An outstanding example of a community website becoming very valuable is Groupon.com. In about a year, Groupon went from nothing to getting a six-billion dollar corporate acquisition offer from Google, which they declined by the way. It was the members adding content to the groupon.com website that made the website valuable for its owners.

If Facebook.com were to be acquired by Microsoft.com tomorrow for twenty billion dollars, how much of that twenty billion dollars would each Facebook member receive? The answer is *they would receive nothing.*

Here are just two of the countless examples on the Internet of where people add value to others' domain names.

1. Ning.com offers would-be website owners the ability to assemble a community website – for example rockstar.ning.com – but each such community website is a subdomain of the ning.com website! So, the owners of Ning can eject you and your "website" any time they feel like it. True, you can opt to use you own domain name to point to it instead, but most people don't do this, because they don't understand what is at stake.

2. Blogspot.com is another "free" service that allows people to set up their own blog (e.g. fptp.blogspot.com). Here, too, the owners (Google, in this case, because they own the domain blogspot.com) have final say over whether your blog lives of dies. That is, if you forget to use your own domain name instead of a subdomain name of blogspot.com.

Be afraid. Be very afraid

You've probably heard of Wikileaks and all the fuss about the documents they make available to the public. Even though Wikileaks owns[35] their domain names, and despite the fact that no one had proven Wikileaks had done anything wrong (as of writing this), pressure was brought to

---

35 The government actually owns all of the domain names out there. A handful of organizations are licensed to "rent" domain names to individuals on a year to year basis. But for the purposes of this topic, a person can "own" their domain name.

bear on several companies to shut down Wikileaks' various websites and their means of collecting payments. The fact is, once you publish your website on a hosting company's servers – which by definition, now places your intellectual property (IP) in what is called *The Cloud* - you must understand, they can shut your website down if they feel it is in their interests to do so. Perhaps your political views don't match theirs, or you have upset the government, and so on.

Here is a snippet from an April 2011 article on Aljazeera.net:

"... the attack of WikiLeaks ought to be a wake-up call for anyone who has rosy fantasies about whose side cloud computing providers are on. The 'Terms and Conditions' under which they provide both 'free' and paid-for services will always give them grounds for dropping your content if they deem it in their interests to do so. Put not your faith in cloud computing: it will one day rain on your parade."

Be aware that your website can be shut down without even so much as a court order. That's one of the dirty little secrets of the Internet. Individual web hosting companies – even though you own your own domain name – can pull the plug on your website if they have reason to.

Most organizations will never need to worry about a hosting company pulling the plug on their website. In fact, hosting companies pride themselves on the utter reliability of their service. It is just something to be aware of if you are planning to … well … cause trouble.

You have probably worried on and off about losing the contents of your notebook computer or your iPad. You might have even signed up for an automatic backup service to protect it in the case of loss, but no one has ever asked me if their website was backed up. As it turns out, any good hosting company does actually back up the contents of websites it hosts. It usually doesn't back it up on a moment by moment basis, but more often does a rough weekly backup, which would limit your data risk in the event of a complete disaster. Still, I recommend you get hold of your web developer and ask the question nonetheless: *Is my website backed up*?

Am I safe when I surf the Internet?

People are definitely more wary today than they were a few decades ago about what they type into an email or publish on the Web. We know that, at least, an email sent today may be presented to us years later, perhaps in a divorce hearing or a political campaign. We see in the news that it does happen to politicians, or would-be candidates for office, where an indiscreet email from years ago surfaces to embarrass the politician two days before the election. *There goes my planned run for office,* I hear you say.

I have a rule about Internet security. I never type something on a keyboard that I don't want to see on the front cover of the Seattle Times. I am typing this into my laptop as I sit in a public library, and that laptop is connected to the Internet via the library's unsecured wireless service. Is my laptop somehow viewable by others who are also connected to that open wireless? I have no idea. There must be some software package available on the market that allows someone to snoop or sniff computers using an open wireless. I am guessing, if I don't take actual steps to encrypt my communications over an open wireless, it is relatively easy for someone to examine the transmissions going back and forth.

When you visit a website using a browser[36], you can see if your communications with the website are "secure" or not. Without going into it in great technical detail, a rule of thumb is as follows: If the address bar of your browser begins with http://, it is not secure; if it begins with https://, it is secure. Note the only difference is the letter 's' suffixed to the http at the beginning of the address. The 's' signifies that a Secured Sockets Layer[37] is being used by the server to protect communications going back and forth. Any place on the Web where you enter sensitive data (for example, your credit card details or your social security number) make sure the web address begins with https://.

How secure are my email and password?

Consider this scenario: You accidentally click 'Yes' on some message box that pops up while you are visiting a website on the Internet. Perhaps you are on the phone or watching TV at the time, or perhaps you've had a couple of glasses of wine and are tired after a long day's work. Whatever the excuse you have for pressing that 'Yes' button, you have inadvertently agreed to install a certain piece of software on your copy on Microsoft Windows. You don't even notice that it has happened, although you might get a tad nervous when it says "Acme-thing has been successfully installed!". You forget about the puzzling message for the moment and continue with what you were doing.

---

36 Examples of browsers: Internet Explorer, Firefox, Safari, Google Chrome, Epiphany.
37 Secured Sockets Layer: an extra piece of software that prevents communications over the Internet from being hacked.

What has happened, without you noticing, is that a piece of Spyware[38] was installed and is running inside your personal copy of Windows. The spyware was written to monitor your activity and/or extract data from your laptop and send it to someone without you knowing it. It might wait for you to type your email and password (if it is what is called a "keyboard sniffer") and transmit that to some clandestine location on the Web, or it might scour your email folders looking for social security numbers, credit card details, bank account login info or any other potentially valuable piece of data.

Meanwhile, a team of criminals half way round the world receives your sensitive information (email plus password, social security number, bank account login details, whatever) and they spring into action.

They may begin by locking you out of your own account simply by changing the password. They may thwart your every effort to recover it, and all the while, continue to send out emails to all your contacts with a request for money to be sent to an account somewhere. That's just the damage they can do using your email, and they've done all that before you even got out of bed. You can only imagine what could happen if they can log into your bank account or other assets. It is more than just your identity they can steal.

Microsoft Windows is obviously a very powerful piece of software. Its open installation architecture has allowed thousands of third party software vendors to expand the power of Windows beyond even the wildest dreams of Bill Gates. But that open architecture – the flexible and

---

38

comfortable nature we've all experienced on Windows over the decades – can be taken advantage of by unscrupulous criminals.

Apple laptops are more secure than Windows in that respect, simply because there are fewer of them out there and thus attract less criminal interest, and they do not have the same open architecture as Windows does. Still, there is no such thing as a 100% secure personal computer. Doing the basics to limit the chances of a data theft catastrophe is easy:

1. Make sure your PC is backed up regularly, preferably over the Internet, with encryption. Even if you are careful, someone else might spill a *mocha vente latte* onto your computer, so you might need a way to recover all of its data in the event of a total loss.

2. Never type credit card details, social security numbers or valuable login information into an email. Even if *your* email system is secure (which it isn't, by the way), a recipient's email might get broken into.

3. Never enter sensitive or private information into a website if the address does not begin with **https://**.

4. Use effective passwords. I like a password that has mixed letters, capitalization, numbers and characters, all unrelated to one another. For example, **Reagan1980!** is a poor password because it could be guessed, but **rEagan24x7#** would not be guessed and is therefore a stronger password. There are lots of resources on the Web to help you come

up with a good password. You want one that you can remember easily but would never be guessed.

5. Pay attention to the address bar on your browser. Always know what site you are visiting and beware of Phishing[39]. You might think you are logging into your gmail account, but perhaps the domain name is www.gmaill.com (two Ls) and it is phishing for your email and password.

I believe the children are our future

Cyber-criminals take advantage of the fact that many people share their personal computers with their children. An eight year-old, while impressive with her dexterity with computer mice and game controllers, is easy prey for online criminals. Because she has no fear (at least, when it comes to data security on your laptop) she falls for the most rudimentary attempts by websites to install software on your laptop. What is the moral of this story? Don't share your computer with children, unless you don't care about the data on it. If you do share, at least it will make a great story to tell at his or her wedding – *the day little Johnny lost all the data on my laptop.*

Don't share your computer with children

On a number of occasions, I have noticed a friend or acquaintance online – for example, in Facebook, Gmail, etc. - so I pinged them with a message like "*Hi Joe, how's it going?*" only to be greeted by their son or daughter who

---

39 Phishing, according to Wikipedia: The practice of using fraudulent e-mails and copies of legitimate websites to extract financial data from computer users for purposes of identity theft

is currently using their computer. The response might come back as "oh, dad is out getting a haircut" or, more frighteningly, "dad won't be back from Oslo until Tuesday". Clearly, their dad has left his email open and the child is now using the computer, possibly to play on the Internet or do their homework. Setting aside for a moment the risk to the actual child – and I could write a chapter on how dangerous the Internet is for children – this is a recipe for a data security disaster.

The disaster unfolds like this:
A pop-up message appears, your fearless child clicks Yes, and ten seconds later, a program is scanning your entire computer for sensitive information, before sending it on its merry way across the Interwebs[40]. Your child doesn't even notice that his dad is about to get a second haircut.

I'd sooner give my eleven year-old the keys to my car, than share a laptop with him that runs Microsoft Windows. And he's a good kid.

The Internet equivalent of safe sex

You've probably heard of the Linux operating system. It is based on what they call open source, meaning lots of volunteers have contributed to making it a complete operating system for use for free by anyone who wants it. There are a few "desktop" versions available, meaning you can install Linux on your laptop[41] and use it instead of

---

40 Interwebs: a term coined by George W. Bush during the 2004 presidential debates.
41 You do need some technical expertise to do it right. Ask someone who has done it before to help you.

using the more popular Microsoft Windows operating system.

One of the marvelous things about Linux is, as of writing this, it is not subject to computer viruses or spyware in the way Microsoft Windows is. Still, like anything made by humans, it is not 100% secure. Nothing is.

An Apple Macintosh is more secure than Windows, and the average desktop version of Linux is more secure than either of them. Why? Microsoft Windows is based on an open file directory foundation that is subject to conflicts between different vendors' applications using similar objects each installed on the computer. In addition, its proprietary source code means that no one but Microsoft is in a real position to fix a security leak, whereas millions of people can take all day to find those security leaks and exploit them before Microsoft even knows about them.

The Linux operating system – by its very nature as an open source program – has thousands of programmers looking for weaknesses in the source code itself and submitting fixes to the open source community before they can be taken advantage of. That might sound like a contradiction – source code being public making it more secure – but in actual practice, it makes for a far more secure operating system. Sunlight, it seems, does make a great disinfectant.

On top of the operating system, you need applications of course, and there are thousands of free-to-use business applications – alternatives to everything from Microsoft Office to Adobe Photoshop – available for immediate download and use by anyone running such a Linux operating system. And all of the files you create are interchangeable with Microsoft Office files.

I am typing this book in OpenOffice Writer version 3.2 on a Linux-Ubuntu desktop operating system version 10.
Who knew!

Safety in numbers

Thankfully, most of us never experience a serious security problem with the data on our personal computer. It is not because it is secure. It is because there is a vast ocean of easy targets out there for criminals to focus on. The law of the herd at least gives you safety in numbers.

Most small businesses these days need to use a lot of this new Internet technology to run their business, so they can't protect themselves simply by not using the technology. In addition, it's usually difficult to depart from the use of Microsoft Windows because you would have to train your staff on a new set of software programs. It might not be worth it. Still, you can reduce your chances of a disaster (on any laptop or personal computer) by an order of magnitude by following the simple security steps listed on page 177.

Getting help

Who will build your website?

Most business owners are not in a position to build their own website by hand. At least, not a website that will represent and serve their company well enough. In the past, an organization's web presence was as important as last year's marketing brochure. Today, in the second decade of the twenty first century, an organization's web presence is critical to survival. You might have technical skills on your team, even a person or people who have built websites before, but it may not be enough, because the tools and skills become obsolete so quickly.

It may be preferable to hire an organization that specializes in developing a professional web presence for its clients, rather than trying to do it all internally.

Among the skills needed to develop a web presence are knowledge and experience in the following areas:

- Search Engine Optimization
- At least one Content Management System (WordPress, Drupal, Joomla, ExpressionEngine, etc.)
- Social Media tools (Facebook, Twitter, etc.)
- Website design
- Image manipulation (Photoshop, Gimp, Paintshop Pro, etc.)
- Content creation.

This list is not in any particular order because the relative importance of its items will vary depending on what business you are in. If your target market is people in their sixties or older, you are unlikely to find them on Twitter, but if you are selling tutorial services to teenagers, your Twitter account – and your entire Social Media effort – may be central to your efforts. Then again, it may not be. It depends on where the purchase decision makers for your target market live. Only you can know that.

People in business generally know other people in business. A few phone calls to your fellow businesspeople and you will likely have a shortlist of potential vendors who can deliver the web presence you need.

Page 184

Bricks to Clicks

Page 184

Chapter 11 - Wrapping up

Well, you've made it this far. I really hope there was something of use to you in this book. I never claim to have all the answers, because I know I learn something new every day. Sometimes I learn that I've been flat wrong.

I have always been able to answer questions my readers send me. People often express surprise when I respond in person to questions in email, but I tell them, I just don't get the volume of questions I would expect for all the books that people buy. So please send your question to liam.scanlan@gmail.com

Something special

Visit this book's website at the following unpublished location, where I offer a special offer to readers of this book:
www.sboseries.com/specials

In the meantime, I wish you the very best of good fortune in your journey to success on the Internet.

Keep in touch.

Liam Scanlan

Seattle, Washington

Alphabetical Index

Bricks to Clicks

www.ingramcontent.com/pod-product-compliance
Lightning Source LLC
Chambersburg PA
CBHW071152050326
40689CB00011B/2075